SAINT FRANCIS OF ASSISI
HIS ESSENTIAL WISDOM

SAINT FRANCIS OF ASSISI
HIS ESSENTIAL WISDOM

Edited by CAROL KELLY-GANGI

FALL RIVER PRESS

To Mom and Dad Gangi with love.

Compilation © 2010 by Carol Kelly-Gangi

Book design by Lundquist Design

Fall River Press
122 Fifth Avenue
New York, NY 10011

ISBN: 978-1-4351-2311-3

Printed and bound in the United States of America

10 9 8 7 6 5 4 3 2 1

CONTENTS

INTRODUCTION

St. Francis of Assisi spent the first twenty-four years of his life in an unremarkable way. He was born in 1181 to a wealthy cloth merchant, Pietro Bernardone, and his wife Pica. Pietro was away on business in France when their child was born, so Pica had him baptized Giovanni, after John the Baptist. Upon his return, Pietro was enraged by her choice of name. A name that recalled the poor, wild herald of Christ was certainly not suitable for the son of a respectable merchant. Instead, Pietro took to calling his son Francesco, possibly to celebrate his successful business dealings in France.

By all accounts, Francis grew up to be an amiable young man, albeit a wastrel, who enjoyed fashionable clothes, parties with friends, and all of the amusements available to a young man of his class in Assisi. Yet several key events in Francis's life set him on a dramatically different course. Among these is the time he spent in prison.

At the age of twenty, Francis fought in a war between Assisi and neighboring Perugia. When Assisi was defeated, Francis was taken prisoner by the Perugian forces, and he spent a year imprisoned in a damp dungeon, in almost total darkness, subsisting on a diet of stale bread and foul water. For the first time in his privileged life, he suffered deprivations and misery. Yet, despite the deplorable conditions, he retained his good nature, and the concern he displayed for the less fortunate among them became apparent to his fellow prisoners. During his imprisonment he contracted an illness, possibly malaria or tuberculosis, and returned to Assisi in a weakened condition.

Within two years, however, still aspiring to a career as a knight, Francis embarked on yet another military campaign, this time with the papal forces led by Walter de Brienne. He stopped for the night twenty miles outside of Assisi and his illness returned. During the night, he had a startling vision that moved him to return to Assisi and try to ascertain his true vocation. Having lost interest in business, his friends and their former pursuits, Francis started to search for some deeper meaning to his life.

In the spring of 1206 Francis stopped at a dilapidated church in San Damiano to pray. While kneeling and contemplating the crucifix, Francis heard the voice of God imploring him, "Francis, don't you see that my house has collapsed? Go and repair it for me." Francis accepted God's challenge and immediately went about selling his horse, his clothes, and bolts of his father's cloth and gave the proceeds to the priest at San Damiano. Knowing his father would be outraged, Francis hid in a cave for weeks.

Eventually he returned to Assisi, looking wild and haggard, to face his father's wrath. Pietro dragged Francis home and locked him in the cellar, but Pica released him while Pietro was away.

Finally, Pietro turned to the bishop for a judgment against his son. In a dramatic public trial in front of the bishop, Francis agreed to give his father back the money that belonged to him, and summarily stripped off all of his clothes and laid them at his father's feet, announcing for all to hear, "Up until now I have always called Pietro Bernardone my father. In the future I will only acknowledge our Father who is in heaven." This is said to be the moment of Francis's final conversion.

The bishop gave Francis some rough clothes and he soon returned to San Damiano to continue his work on the church. He begged for stones for the repairs, singing the praises of God, and began to preach his new way of life based on the Gospel. His first follower, Bernard of Quintavalle, a respected businessman, joined Francis in 1208. Others soon followed, including Brother Giles (later St. Giles of Assisi) and Peter of Cattaneo. Their habit was a simple tunic made of the coarsest, cheapest material tied at the waist with a rope. Living in poverty and humility, they begged for food and preached the Gospel. In 1210 Francis and his eleven followers met with Pope Innocent III and were granted permission to form the Order of the Friars Minor. Astoundingly, within a few years, the original number of friars had grown to more than five thousand. They wandered the globe, two by two, continuing their mission of preaching, begging, and acting as servants to all.

Two years before his death, St. Francis received the gift of the stigmata—his hands and feet pierced as though with nails and an open wound on his side—mirroring the wounds that Christ received during the crucifixion. Suffering from a dreadful eye disease he had contracted in Egypt when he attempted to convert the sultan, he was nearly blind and gravely ill by the time of his death. And on October 3, 1226, surrounded by his brothers and whispering his prayers, St. Francis died peacefully. He was forty-five years old. Less than two years later, St. Francis was canonized by Pope Gregory IX, who broke down in tears during his eulogy of the great saint.

In testament to his enduring legacy, millions of people make the pilgrimage every year to Assisi to visit the tomb of St. Francis and to feel the presence of this universally beloved saint.

Saint Francis of Assisi: His Essential Wisdom is a collection of more than 300 quotations by and about St. Francis. Many of these selections are drawn from the saint's own writings and those he dictated to his brothers. In simple yet profound language, St. Francis wrote rules and exhortations for his brothers, letters to priests, ministers, and his lay followers, directives to St. Clare and her sisters, as well as heartfelt prayers and blessings. Evident in every word is his deep and abiding love of God and his fervent desire to serve Him and all of creation. His passion is palpable as he praises his Creator, guides his brothers and followers, and sets forth the rules to govern them in their daily lives. Fundamental to these are poverty, which leads them to God; holy humility, which infuses their every action; and absolute obedience and charity to all of humanity. The pinnacle of his praise for the Creator is "The Canticle of Brother Sun," in which he joyfully praises God and all of His creation even in the midst of his own great personal suffering.

Also included are many selections from the early biographies of St. Francis written by Thomas of Celano and St. Bonaventure, as well as excerpts from well-known early Franciscan works such as *The Legend of the Three Companions*, which are the memoirs of Brothers Leo, Angelo, and Rufino, and *The Little Flowers of St. Francis*, which may have been written by a colleague of one of Brother Leo's disciples in the first half of the fourteenth century. In these charming selections, many of St. Francis's miracles are revealed, especially those involving birds, fish, and wild animals, as well as his love and respect for all of nature. Finally, there are excerpts from modern biographies of St. Francis, that help to put his life and works into context for today's readers.

What does a saint who lived some eight hundred years ago have to say that could possibly be relevant to us today? Take the time to revisit St. Francis and his teachings—in all of their profound simplicity—they are here to inspire, guide, challenge, and transform us, now, as they have done for readers through the centuries.

—Carol Kelly-Gangi
Rumson, New Jersey, 2010

A CALL TO SERVE

He gave himself over to amusements and songs and liked to stroll day and night through the city of Assisi with comrades of the same age. In his expenditures he was so liberal that he wasted on parties and other merrymaking everything that he might own or acquire. . . . Always generous, even prodigal, he also lacked moderation in the way that he dressed: he had suits tailored for himself that were much more elegant than his status demanded.

—*The Legend of the Three Companions*

Francis wasted his time miserably, encouraging wickedness until he was nearly twenty-four years old.

—*The First Life of St. Francis* by Thomas of Celano, quoted in *Francis of Assisi: A Revolutionary Life* by Adrian House

One day when Francis was in his father's shop selling cloth, a poor man came in and begged for alms for the love of God. Francis was busy and turned him away. At that moment, the grace of God touched him, and he reproached himself for his hard-heartedness. If the beggar had pleaded in the name of some great lord or noble, he said to himself, I would surely have given him what he asked. How much more willingly should I do so for the sake of the King of Kings, the Lord of creation? From that day he resolved never again to refuse anything that might be asked of him for the love of God.

—*The Wisdom of St. Francis and His Companions* by
Stephen Clissold

You may think me foolish, but one day the whole world will come to respect me.

—St. Francis's comment to a fellow prisoner of war, who was
chiding him for his cheerfulness, quoted in *Francis of Assisi:
A Revolutionary Life* by Adrian House

A Call to Serve

This is how the Lord gave me, Brother Francis, the grace to begin to do penance: when I was yet in my sins, it seemed to me unbearably bitter to see lepers. And the Lord himself led me among them, and I showed kindness toward them. And as I went away from them, that which had seemed bitter to me was now changed for me into sweetness of mind and body. And then I tarried yet a little while, and left the world. And the Lord gave me such a faith in the churches, that in a simple way I would thus pray and say: "We adore You, O Lord Jesus Christ, [here] and in all Your churches which are in the whole world, and we bless You, because by Your holy cross You have redeemed the world."

—*Testament of the Holy Father St. Francis*

Francis, whilst waiting to discover God's will for his life, went to live in a cave and prayed: Who are you, my dear Lord and God, and who am I, your miserable worm of a servant? My dearest Lord, I want to love you. My Lord and my God, I give you my heart and my body, and would wish, if only I knew how, to do still more for the love of you!

—*The Wisdom of St. Francis and His Companions* by Stephen Clissold

Imperceptibly, Francis was detaching himself from his old life, to the baffled indignation of the father who had made very different plans for his son. Francis had set his feet on a new path—but where would it lead? Beggars could be fed, and lepers tended; but how could the crucified Lord of all be served? One day, when kneeling in prayer in the tumble-down chapel of St. Damian's [San Damiano], Francis was given the answer. The figure on the cross seemed to address him with the words: "Francis, repair my church." Trembling with joy and awe, Francis set about fulfilling the command with single-minded zeal.

> —*The Wisdom of St. Francis and His Companions* by
>   Stephen Clissold

From that hour on, compassion for the crucified Christ was imprinted on his holy soul, and one may piously suppose that the sacred stigmata were then deeply engraved in his heart, before being engraved in his flesh. From the moment when he heard the voice of his Beloved, his soul melted with love. He could not henceforth contain his tears and he would moan aloud over the Passion of Christ, which he seemed to have unceasingly before his eyes. He made the byways echo with his lamentations, and while meditating on Christ's wounds he refused to be consoled.

> —*The Second Life of St. Francis* by Thomas of Celano

A Call to Serve

Until this hour I have called Pietro Bernardone my father on earth, from henceforth, I may say confidently, my Father Who art in heaven, in Whose hands I have laid up all my treasures, all my trust, and all my hope.

—St. Francis quoted in *The Life of St. Francis of Assisi* by
St. Bonaventure

I have resolved in my heart to abandon the world and follow you in that which you command.

—St. Francis

He was caught up above himself, and absorbed into a kind of light; the capacity of his mind was enlarged, and he could see clearly into the future. He said to his brothers . . . "I saw a great many men who wanted to share our way of life—the roads, as it were, filled with Frenchmen, Spaniards, Germans, Englishmen and many others, speaking various languages and hurrying toward us."

—describing Francis's vision at a cave in Poggio Bustone in
1208, *The First Life of St. Francis* by Thomas of Celano

I have found a really excellent man who wants to live according to the Gospel, preserving precisely its evangelical spirit. I am convinced our Lord wishes to renew the faith of the holy church, all over the world, through him.

—Cardinal San Paolo to Pope Innocent III about Francis in 1209, *The Legend of the Three Companions*

We approve your rule. Go, Brothers, with the Lord and preach penitence to everyone, in whatever way He inspires you. And when He increases His grace in you and multiplies your numbers, come back and report everything to us. We will then concede more to you, and entrust you with even greater work.

—Pope Innocent III approving St. Francis's Order in 1209, *The Legend of the Three Companions*

And after the Lord had given me brothers, no one showed me what I was to do, but the Most High Himself revealed to me that I should live according to the pattern of the Holy Gospel. And I had it written down in few words and simple manner, and the Lord Pope [Innocent III] confirmed it to me. And those who came to accept this way of life gave to the poor whatever they might have had. And they were content with one habit [cf. Matt. 10:10; Luke 9:3], quilted inside and out, with a cord and breeches. And we had no desire for aught else.

—*Testament of the Holy Father St. Francis*

A Call to Serve

Be comforted, my dearest children, and rejoice in the Lord, and be not troubled because you are so few, nor affrighted by reason of your simplicity, for the Lord has truly shown me that God will make us increase to a great multitude, and will pour forth the grace of His benediction upon us.

> —St. Francis quoted in *The Life of St. Francis of Assisi* by
> St. Bonaventure

He wants you to go about the world preaching, because God did not call you for yourself alone but also for the salvation of others.

> —Brother Masseo's response to St. Francis, who requested his
> companions pray to God for an answer about his ministry,
> from *The Little Flowers of St. Francis*

Go, proclaim peace to men, preach penance for the remission of sins. Be patient in tribulation, watchful in prayer, strong in labor, moderate in speech, grave in conversation, thankful for benefits; for if you shall observe all these things, an eternal kingdom is prepared for you.

> —St. Francis quoted in *The Life of St. Francis of Assisi* by
> St. Bonaventure

He blessed each of the friars, and gave anyone endowed by God with the necessary eloquence permission to preach, whether a priest or a lay brother. Then, in great joy of spirit they started on their way through the world as pilgrims and strangers.

—*The Legend of the Three Companions*

Cast thy care upon the Lord, and He will nourish thee.

—St. Francis's words to every brother, quoted in *The Life of St. Francis* by St. Bonaventure

Have no fear of being thought insignificant or unbalanced, but preach repentance with courage and simplicity. Have faith in the Lord, who has overcome the world. His Spirit speaks in you and through you, calling men and women to turn to Him and observe His precepts.

—St. Francis quoted in *The Legend of the Three Companions*

A Call to Serve

The very sight of him, as they listened to his exhortations, banished any worries they had. He spoke to them not as a judge but as a father to his children. Like a doctor among his patients, he suffered with the sick and grieved with the distressed. Nevertheless he knew how to reprove those who had done wrong and discipline the obstinate or rebellious.

—The early days of the Order described in *The Legend of the Three Companions*

I did not come to be served but to serve (cf. Matt. 10:28), says the Lord. Those who are placed over others should glory in such an office only as much as they would were they assigned the task of washing the feet of the brothers. And the more they are upset about their office being taken from them than they would be over the loss of the office of [washing] feet, so much the more do they store up treasures to the peril of their souls (cf. John 12:6).

—St. Francis, The Admonitions, IV

My dear Brothers, give thanks to Our Lord Jesus Christ who has deigned to reveal the treasures of divine wisdom through the mouths of simple ones. For God is He who opens the mouths of infants and the dumb, and when He wishes, He makes the tongues of the simple speak very wisely.

—St. Francis to his brothers after Christ appeared to them in a vision, from *The Little Flowers of St. Francis*

My brothers, my brothers! God has called me to follow the way of simplicity, and I don't want you to continue pressing some other rule on me—neither St. Augustine's, nor St. Bernard's, nor St. Benedict's. The Lord told me He wished me to be a new kind of fool—and doesn't want us to be guided by any higher learning than that. God will confound you for your knowledge and sagacity and I trust that His constables will punish you for them. Then, to your shame, you will return to your first state.

—St. Francis, in response to pressure from a cardinal to follow a preexisting religious order, from *The Legend of Perugia,* quoted in *Francis of Assisi: A Revolutionary Life* by Adrian House

My little sons, we have promised great things to God, but far greater things have been promised to us by God. Let us keep those promises which we have made, and let us aspire with confidence to those things that have been promised to us. Brief is the world's pleasure, but the punishment that follows it lasts forever. Small is the suffering of this life, but the glory of the next life is infinite.

—St. Francis, speaking at a General Chapter meeting of more than 5,000 friars, from *The Little Flowers of St. Francis*

GOD THE FATHER, THE SON, AND THE HOLY SPIRIT

Oh, how glorious it is, how holy and great, to have a Father in heaven! Oh, how holy, consoling, beautiful, and wondrous it is to have a Spouse in heaven! Oh, how holy and how loving, pleasing, humble, peaceful, sweet, lovable, and desirable above all things to have such a Brother and Son, Who laid down His life for His sheep (cf. John 10:15) and [Who] prayed to the Father for us saying: "Holy Father, protect those in your name whom you have given to me" (cf. John 17:11).

—St. Francis, Letter to All the Faithful, Second Version

And let us render all good things to the Lord God most high and supreme, and acknowledge that all good things are His, and give Him thanks for all from Whom all good things come. And may He, the most High and Supreme, the only true God, have, and may there be rendered to Him and may He receive all honor and reverence, all praises and blessings, all thanks and glory, to whom every good belongs, who alone is good (cf. Luke 18:19).

—St. Francis, Rule of 1221, XVII

Every creature in heaven and on earth and in the depths of the sea should give God praise and glory and honor and blessing; He has borne so much for us and has done and will do so much good to us; He is our power and our strength and He alone is supreme good, He alone most high, He alone all-powerful, wonderful, and glorious; He alone is holy and worthy of all praise and blessing for endless ages and ages. Amen!

—St. Francis, Letter to All the Faithful

Let all of us everywhere, in every place, at every hour, and every season, daily and constantly, truly and humbly believe and hold in our hearts, and love, honor, adore, serve, praise and bless, glorify and exalt, magnify and render thanks to the most High and Supreme Eternal God, Trinity and Unity, the Creator of all and the Savior of all who believe and hope in Him and love Him who, without beginning and without end, is unchangeable, unseen, indescribable, ineffable, incomprehensible, unfathomable, blessed, praiseworthy, glorious, exalted above all, sublime, most high, gentle, lovable, delightful and wholly desirable above all else, for ever. Amen.

—St. Francis, Rule of 1221, XXIII

Everyday, Jesus humbles himself just as He did when He came from His heavenly throne into the Virgin's womb; everyday He comes to us and lets us see Him in abjection, when He descends from the bosom of the Father into the hands of the priest at the altar.

—St. Francis, The Admonitions, I

And as He appeared to the holy apostles in true flesh, so now He reveals Himself to us in the sacred bread. And as they saw only His flesh by means of their bodily sight, yet believed Him to be God as they contemplated Him with the eyes of faith, so, as we see bread and wine with [our] bodily eyes, we too are to see and firmly believe them to be His most holy Body and Blood living and true. And in this way the Lord is always with His faithful, as He Himself says: "Behold I am with you even to the end of the world" (cf. Matt. 28:20).

—St. Francis, The Admonitions, I

I beg you, with all that is in me and more, that, when it is appropriate and you judge it profitable, you humbly beg the clergy to revere above everything else the most holy Body and Blood of our Lord Jesus Christ and His holy written words which consecrate [His] Body.

—St. Francis, Letter to the Custodians

But blessed Christ never hardens the heart of the faithful. On the contrary, He softens it, as He says through the mouth of the prophet, "I will take away your heart of stone and give you a heart of flesh."

—St. Francis

Let all of us, brothers, look to the Good Shepherd Who suffered the passion of the cross to save His sheep. The sheep of the Lord followed Him in tribulation and persecution, in insult and hunger, in infirmity and temptation, and in everything else, and they have received everlasting life from the Lord because of these things. Therefore, it is a great shame for us, servants of God, that while the saints actually did such things, we wish to receive glory and honor by merely recounting their deeds.

—St. Francis, The Admonitions, VI

Therefore, kissing your feet and with all that love of which I am capable, I implore all of you brothers to show all possible reverence and honor to the most holy Body and Blood of our Lord Jesus Christ in Whom that which is in the heavens and on the earth is brought to peace and is reconciled to the all-powerful God (cf. Col. 1:20).

—St. Francis, Letter to the Entire Order

Therefore it is the Spirit of the Lord, Who lives in His faithful, Who receives the most holy Body and Blood of the Lord. All others who do not share in this same Spirit and who presume to receive Him eat and drink judgment to themselves (cf. 1 Cor. 11:29).

—St. Francis, The Admonitions, I

We are spouses when by the Holy Spirit the faithful soul is joined to Jesus Christ; we are brothers to Him when we do the will of the Father Who is in heaven. We are mothers when we carry Him in our hearts and bodies through a divine love and a pure and sincere conscience and give birth to Him through a holy activity that must shine as an example before others (cf. Matt. 5, 16).

—St. Francis, Letter to All the Faithful

LOVE AND JOY

And let us love our neighbors as ourselves, and, if any one does not wish to love them as himself or cannot, let him at least do them no harm, but let him do good to them. Let those who have received the power of judging others, exercise judgment with mercy, as they hope to obtain mercy from the Lord.

—St. Francis, Letter to All the Faithful

Each one should confidently make known his need to the other, so that he might find what he needs and minister to him. And each one should love and care for his brother in all those things in which God will give him grace, as a mother loves and cares for her son. (cf. 1 Thess. 2:7).

—St. Francis, Rule of 1221, XI

The Lord says: "Love your enemies [do good to those who

hate you, and pray for those who persecute and blame you]"
(cf. Matt. 5:44). That person truly loves his enemy who is not
upset at any injury which is done to himself, but out of love
of God is disturbed at the sin on the other's soul. And let him
show his love for the other by his deeds.

—St. Francis, The Admonitions, IX

Blessed is the servant who would love his brother as much when
his is sick and cannot repay him as he would when he is well and
can repay him.

—St. Francis, The Admonitions, XXV

It is not fitting, when one is in God's service, to have a gloomy
face or a chilling look.

—St. Francis

The safest remedy against the thousand snares and wiles of the
enemy is spiritual joy.

—St. Francis, *The Second Life of St. Francis* by Thomas of Celano

LOVE AND JOY

I return from Perugia and arrive here in the dead of night; and it is wintertime, muddy and so cold that icicles have formed on the edges of my habit and keep striking my legs, and blood flows from such wounds. And all covered with mud and cold, I come to the gate and after I have knocked and called for some time, a brother comes and asks: "Who are you?" I answer: "Brother Francis," And he says, "Go away; this is not a proper hour for going about; you may not come in." And when I insist, he answers: "Go away, you are a simple and a stupid person; we are so many and we have no need of you. You are certainly not coming to us at this hour." And I stand again at the door and say, "For the love of God, take me in tonight." And he answers: "I will not. Go to the Crosier's place and ask there." I tell you this: If I had patience and did not become upset, there would be true joy in this, and true virtue and the salvation of the soul.

—St. Francis, quoted in *The Second Life of St. Francis* by
　　Thomas of Celano

For what else are the servants of God than his singers, whose duty it is to lift up the hearts of men and move them to spiritual joy?

—St. Francis

THE RELIGIOUS LIFE

We have been called to heal wounds, to unite what has fallen apart, and to bring home those who have lost their way.

—St. Francis

Chaste embraces, gentle feelings, a holy kiss, pleasing conversation, modest laughter, joyous looks, a single eye, a submissive spirit, a peaceable tongue, a mild answer, oneness of purpose, ready obedience, unwearied hand, all these were found in them.

—*The First Life of St. Francis* by Thomas of Celano

The Rule and life of these brothers is this, namely to live in obedience, in chastity, and without anything of their own, and to follow the teaching and the footsteps of Our Lord Jesus Christ, who says: "if thou wilt be perfect, go and sell all that thou hast and give to the poor, and thou shalt have treasure in heaven; and come, follow Me" (cf. Matt. 19:21). And: "If any one will come after Me, let him deny himself and take up his cross and follow Me" (cf. Matt. 16:24). In like manner: "If any one wishes to come to Me, and does not hate father and mother and wife and children and brothers and sisters, yes and his own life also, cannot be My disciple" (cf. Luke 14:26). And: "Everyone who has left father and mother, brothers or sisters, wife or children, houses or lands for My sake, shall receive a hundred-fold and shall possess life everlasting" (cf. Matt. 19:29; Mark 10:29–30; Luke 18:29)

—St. Francis, The Rule of 1221, I

If anyone wishing by divine inspiration to embrace this life should come to our brothers, let him be received kindly by them. And if he be firmly resolved to accept our life, let the brothers take great care not to meddle with his temporal affairs, but present him as soon as possible to their minister. The minister is to receive him kindly and encourage him and carefully explain to him the tenor of our life. Thereupon, if he be willing and able, in conscience and without hindrance, he is to sell all his goods and endeavor to distribute them to the poor. The brothers and the minister of the brothers are to take care not to interfere in any way in his affairs, nor are they to receive any money, either themselves or through a middleman. If however they are in want, the brothers can receive other material necessities, except money, by reason of their needs, like other poor people. And when he has returned, the minister is to give him the clothes of probation for a year, namely two tunics without a hood, and a cord, and breeches and a small cape reaching to the cord. When the year and term of probation is ended, let him be received to obedience. Thereafter it shall not be lawful for him to pass to another Order nor to "wander about beyond obedience," according to the command of the Lord Pope and the Gospel, for "no man putting his hand to the plow and looking back, is fit for the kingdom of God" (Luke 9:62).

—St. Francis, Rule of 1221, II

The Rule and Life of the Friars Minor is this: to observe the Holy Gospel of our Lord Jesus Christ through a life in obedience, without anything of their own, and in chastity. Brother Francis promises obedience and reverence to the Lord Pope Honorius and to his lawful successors, and to the Roman Church. And the other friars are to be bound to give obedience to Brother Francis and to his successors.

—St. Francis, Final Rule of the Friars Minor 1223, I

Should any persons come to the friars with the desire to adopt this way of life, they are to be directed to their ministers provincial. Only to the latter and to none other may the power be granted to receive new brethren. On their part, let the ministers subject such persons to a most careful examination on the Catholic faith and the Sacraments of the Church. They must be found to have true belief in all these matters, and the firm intention to profess loyally what they believe and steadfastly to conform their whole life long to such beliefs.

—St. Francis, Final Rule of the Friars Minor 1223, II

And by no manner or means shall they be allowed to leave this Order, both because the Pope has forbidden them and because according to the Holy Gospel: "No one, having put his hand to the plow and looking back, is fit for the kingdom of God." And those who have already promised obedience are to have one tunic with a hood; and, if they wish, a second without a hood. And those who are in need thereof may wear shoes. And all the friars are to wear clothing inferior in quality and appearance; and with the blessing of God they may quilt them with pieces of sack or other material.

—St. Francis, Final Rule of the Friars Minor 1223, II

But I counsel my friars, warn and beseech them in the Lord Jesus Christ, that when they go among other men in the world they do not quarrel or bicker or criticize others. Rather, it is their duty to be mild, peaceful and unassuming, calm and humble; and their words, no matter with whom they are speaking, must always be respectful of the other person. And they are not to ride horseback, save when required by evident necessity or infirmity. Into whatever house they enter, let them first say: "Peace to this house." And according to the Holy Gospel, they are free to eat of whatever food is set before them.

—St. Francis, Final Rule of the Friars Minor 1223, III

I strictly command the friars, each and all, never under any circumstances to take money, whether it be in the form of coins or of gold, either directly themselves or through some person acting as intermediary. But for the needs of the sick and for the clothing of the other friars, it shall be the duty of the ministers and custodes, and theirs alone, to turn to spiritual friends and with their help to provide what is needed. In this they will take into account the circumstances which can arise from such things as the diversity of places, the season of the year, and the cold climate. They may do whatever they feel is called for by the necessity, but always with the one condition made above, that they do not receive money in any form.

—St. Francis, Final Rule of the Friars Minor 1223, IV

Those Brothers who are blessed by the Lord with ability in some form of work, should do their work faithfully and out of a sense of dedication. In this way they will put to rout that enemy of the soul, idleness; and at the same time not destroy the spirit of holy prayer and devotedness. For to this inner spirit all other things of life should positively contribute. As pay for their work, they may receive things needed for bodily sustenance, for themselves or their brethren, but not money in any form. In this let them act in all humility, as befits men who are the servants of God and followers of most holy poverty.

—St. Francis, Final Rule of the Friars Minor 1223, V

I would have my brethren to labor and strive, and not to give place by idleness to unlawful thoughts or idle words.

—St. Francis, quoted in *The Life of St. Francis of Assisi* by St. Bonaventure

The friars are to take nothing as their own, whether it be a house, or a place, or anything at all. Instead, they are to be as pilgrims and strangers in this world; and as those who serve the Lord in poverty and lowliness, let them go begging for alms with full hope in Him. Nor should they feel shame thereby, since for our sakes the Lord himself came into this world as a poor man. Such indeed is the greatness of this perfect poverty that it makes you, my dearest brothers, heirs and kings of the kingdom of heaven, so that though you are thereby in want of this world's good you are made rich in virtues. Let this always be your "portion" here below, for it will bring you to "the land of the living." Hold fast to it, most beloved brothers, with all your soul, and never desire to have aught else under heaven, for the sake of our Lord Jesus Christ. (cf. Ps. 142:5) And wherever the friars may be together or come upon any of their brethren, let them show by their behavior toward one another that they are all of one family. And if one of them is in need, he should in full freedom and trust make known that need to the other. For if a mother has such care and love for the child born of her flesh, how much more love and care must not one have for him who is his brother according to the Spirit? And if any of them becomes sick, the other friars are to take that care of him which they would wish to have themselves.

—St. Francis, Final Rule of the Friars Minor 1223, VI

None of the friars assembled at the chapter ever dared to recount any worldly events; they spoke together of the lives of the holy fathers of old, and how they might best live in God's grace.

—*The Legend of the Three Companions*

If quiet is needed to eat the bread of the body, which, with what it eats, shall become the food of worms, with how far greater peace and tranquility ought the soul to receive the nourishment of its life!

—St. Francis, quoted in *The Life of St. Francis of Assisi* by St. Bonaventure

Blessed is the servant who, when he speaks, does not reveal everything about himself in the hope of receiving a reward, and who is not quick to speak (cf. Prov. 29:20), but wisely weighs what he should say and how he should reply. Woe to that religious who does not keep in his heart the good things the Lord reveals to him (cf. Luke 2:19, 51) and who does not manifest them to others by his actions, but rather seeks to make such good things known by his words. He thereby receives his reward (cf. Matt. 6:2, 16) while those who listen to him carry away but little fruit.

—St. Francis, The Admonitions, XXI

Blessed is the servant who would love and respect his brother as much when he is far from him as he would when he is with him, and who would not say anything behind his back which in charity he could not say to his face.

—St. Francis, The Admonitions, XXV

My office of governing the brothers is spiritual, in that I must overcome and correct vices. If I cannot do this by my preaching and example, then I surely do not want to do it like a taskmaster, beating and flogging the brothers the way a worldly master does.

—St. Francis quoted in *The Legend of the Three Companions*

Be off with you, Brother Fly. You are like an idle drone, living off the other bees' harvest.

—St. Francis dismisses a brother for failure to pray and work sufficiently, from "The Legend of Perugia"

Brother Leo, [wish] your Brother Francis health and peace! I speak to you, my son, as a mother. I place all the words which we spoke on the road in this phrase, briefly and [as] advice. And afterwards, if it is necessary for you to come to me for counsel, I say this to you: In whatever way it seems best to you to please the Lord God and to follow His footprints and His poverty, do this with the blessing of God and my obedience. And if you believe it necessary for the well-being of your soul, or to find comfort, and you wish to come to me, Leo, come!

—St. Francis's letter to Brother Leo, from *Francis and Clare: The Complete Works* edited by Regis J. Armstrong and Ignatius Brady

The preacher must first draw from his secret prayers what he will later pour out in holy sermons; he must grow hot within before he speaks words that are cold in themselves.

—St. Francis quoted in *The Second Life of St. Francis* by Thomas of Celano

Those thus appointed I advise and beseech that in their preaching they use words that are well chosen and chaste, to instruct and edify the people. Let them speak to them of vices and virtues, punishment and glory, in a discourse that is brief, because it was in few words that the Lord preached while on earth.

—St. Francis, Final Rule of the Friars Minor 1223, IX

Brother Francis [sends his] wishes of health to Brother Anthony, my bishop. It pleases me that you teach sacred theology to the brothers, as long as—in the words of the Rule—you "do not extinguish the Spirit of prayer and devotion" with study of this kind.

—St. Francis, Letter to St. Anthony

My Lord, my friars have been called minors that they might not presume to become majors. If thou wilt have them to bear fruit in the Church of God, keep and preserve them in this their state and vocation, and never suffer them to rise to ecclesiastical prelatures.

—St. Francis declines the request of the Cardinal of Ostia— later Pope Gregory IX—to promote some of the Friars Minor

Those who wish to live the gospel life in hermitages are to be three brothers or four at most. Two of them are to be the "mothers" and have two "sons" or one at least. Those who are mothers are to lead the life of Martha, and the two sons are to follow the life of Mary (cf. Luke 10:38-42) and are to have an enclosure in which each one shall have his cell in which he is to pray and sleep.

—St. Francis, The Rule for Hermitages

Those friars who are the "mothers" are to take care to keep apart from any outsiders; and in obedience to their minister are to guard their "sons" from every outside contact, so that no one can speak with them. And the "sons" are not to speak with any person save with their "mothers" and with their minister or custos [regional superior] when it shall please them to visit the "sons" with the blessing of the Lord. From time to time the "sons" are to assume the role of "mothers," taking turns as they have mutually decided. In this, let them faithfully and carefully observe all that is laid down above.

—St. Francis, The Rule for Hermitages

Since by divine inspiration you have made yourselves daughters and servants of the most high King, the heavenly Father, and have taken the Holy Spirit as your spouse, choosing to live according to the perfection of the holy Gospel, I resolve and promise for myself and for my brothers always to have the same loving care and special solicitude for you as [I have] for them.

—St. Francis's Formula for Life, given to Saint Clare and her sisters in 1212

Listen, little poor ones called by the Lord,
    who have come together from many parts and provinces:
Live always in truth,
    that you may die in obedience.
Do not look at the life outside,
    for that of the Spirit is better.
I beg you through great love,
    to use with discretion
    the alms which the Lord gives you.
Those who are weighed down by sickness
    and the others who are wearied because of them,
    all of you: bear it in peace.
For you will sell this fatigue at a very high price
    and each one [of you] will be crowned queen
    in heaven with the Virgin Mary.

  —The Canticle of Exhortation to St. Clare and Her Sisters,
     written by St. Francis to give comfort and encouragement
     to St. Clare and her Poor Ladies of San Damiano

I, the little brother, Francis, wish to live according to the life and poverty of our most exalted Lord, Jesus Christ, and of his most holy Mother, and to continue in this until the end. And, my ladies, I beg and exhort you always to live in this most holy life and poverty. Keep careful watch over yourselves, so that you never abandon it as a result of the teaching or advice of anyone.

  —Last Will and Testament of St. Francis, given to St. Clare
     and her sisters shortly before his death

POVERTY, HUMILITY, CHARITY, AND OBEDIENCE

If we owned anything, we should have to have weapons to protect ourselves. That is what gives rise to contentions and lawsuits, and so often causes the love of God and neighbor to be interfered with. For ourselves, we are resolved to possess nothing temporal in this world.

—St. Francis quoted in *The Legend of the Three Companions*

My dear and beloved Brother, the treasure of blessed poverty is so very precious and divine that we are not worthy to possess it in our vile bodies. For poverty is that heavenly virtue by which all earthly and transitory things are trodden under foot, and by which every obstacle is removed from the soul so that it may freely enter into union with the eternal Lord God. It is also the virtue which makes the soul, while still here on earth, converse with the angels in heaven. It is she who accompanied Christ on the Cross, was buried with Christ in the Tomb, and with Christ was raised and ascended into heaven, for even in this life she gives to souls who love her the ability to fly to heaven, and she alone guards the armor of true humility and charity. So let us pray to the very holy Apostles of Christ, who were prefect lovers of the pearl of the Gospel, that they may procure this grace for us from Our Lord Jesus Christ: that He who was an observer and teacher of holy poverty may by His most holy mercy grant that we may be worthy to be true lovers and observers and humble followers of the most precious and beloved poverty of the Gospel.

—St. Francis, from *The Little Flowers of St. Francis*

When the Brothers go through the world they are to carry nothing for the journey, neither a sack, nor scrip, nor bread, nor money, nor staff.

—St. Francis, Rule of 1221, XIV

We must be firmly convinced that we have nothing of our own, except our vices and sins.

—St. Francis, Rule of 1221, XVII

Grant me the treasure of sublime poverty: permit the distinctive sign of our order to be that it does not possess anything of its own beneath the sun, for the glory of your name, and that it have no other patrimony than begging.

—St. Francis

That is what I consider a great treasure—where nothing has been prepared by human labor. But everything here has been supplied by Divine Providence, as is evident in the begged bread, the fine stone table, and the clear spring. Therefore, I want us to pray to God that He may make us love with all our hearts the very noble treasure of holy poverty, which has God as provider.

—St. Francis, *The Little Flowers of St. Francis*

The friars should make sure that they do not receive under any circumstances churches, houses however small and mean, and all else built for their use, unless these are truly in keeping with the holy poverty we have promised in the Rule; and, as strangers and pilgrims (cf. 1 Pet. 2:11), they should always consider themselves as guests therein.

—*Testament of the Holy Father St. Francis*

All the brothers are to strive to follow the humility and poverty of Our Lord Jesus Christ, and keep in mind that it behooves us to have nothing else in the whole world save that, as the Apostle says: "Having food and clothing, we have all that we need" (cf. 1 Tim. 6:8).

And they should rejoice when they live among persons who are lowly and despised, among the poor and the weak and the sick and the lepers and the beggars by the wayside. And when it should be necessary, let them go for alms. And they should not be ashamed and rather recall to mind that Our Lord Jesus Christ, the Son of the Living God (cf. John 11: 27), set His face like flint (cf. Isa. 50:7) and was not ashamed. And he was poor and a stranger and lived on alms, Himself and the Blessed Virgin and His disciples. And should people treat them with contempt and refuse to give them alms, let them thank God for this, because for such shameful treatment they shall receive great honor before the judgment seat of Our Lord Jesus Christ. And let them realize that such shame is to the discredit of those who inflict it, not of those who suffer it. Moreover, an alms is an inheritance and a right which is due the poor, which Our Lord Jesus Christ gained for us.

—St. Francis, The Rule of 1221, IX

Poverty, Humility, Charity, and Obedience

Know, my brethren, that poverty is the special way to salvation; for it is the food of humility, and the root of perfection, whose fruits, although hidden, are manifold. This is the treasure of which we read in Gospel, which was hidden in the field; to buy which a man should sell all that he hath, and in comparison with which all that can be given for its purchase is to be accounted as nothing. And he who would attain to this height of perfection must lay aside not only worldly prudence, but even all knowledge of letters, that thus stripped of all things he may come to see what is the power of the Lord, and cast himself naked into the arms of the Crucified. Neither does he perfectly renounce the world who keeps a place for the indulgence of his own sense in the secret of his heart.

—St. Francis, *The Life of St. Francis of Assisi* by St. Bonaventure

You can be sure that the more we despise poverty, the more will the world despise us and the greater need will we suffer. But if we embrace holy poverty very closely, the world will come to us and will feed us abundantly. God has called us to this holy Order for the salvation of the world. And He has made this contract between us and the world: that we give the world a good example and that the world provide us with what we need. So let us persevere in holy poverty, because it is the way of perfection and the pledge and guarantee of everlasting riches.

—St. Francis to his brothers, from *The Little Flowers of St. Francis*

Go thy way, Brother Fly, for thou hast in no wise gone forth from thy kindred and from thy father's house. Thou hast given thy goods to thy family, and hast defrauded the poor; thou are not worthy to be a follower of holy poverty. Thou hast begun with the flesh, and hast sought to raise a spiritual building upon a ruinous foundation.

—St. Francis dismisses a man who'd asked to be received into the Order but gave his property to his family rather than to the poor, from *The Life of St. Francis of Assisi* by St. Bonaventure

You want to know why it should be me the world is running after? This is granted me because the eyes of the most high God, which look upon the good and the evil in every place, could not find among sinners anyone more vile, worthless, and sinful than me, or any baser creature on earth for the marvelous work He intends to perform. So He has chosen me to confound the nobility, the greatness, the power, the beauty, and the wisdom of the world. He has done this that men may understand that all virtue and all good proceed from Him alone, and not from any creature.

—St. Francis, from *The Little Flowers of St. Francis*

Poverty, Humility, Charity, and Obedience

The servant of God cannot know how much patience and humility he has within himself as long as everything goes well with him. But when the time comes in which those who should do him justice do quite the opposite to him, he has only as much patience and humility as he has on that occasion and no more.

—St. Francis, The Admonitions, XIII

Blessed are the poor in spirit, for the kingdom of heaven is theirs (cf. Matt. 5:3). There are many who, applying themselves insistently to prayers and good deeds, engage in much abstinence and many mortifications of their bodies, but they are scandalized and quickly roused to anger by a single word which seems injurious to their person, or by some other things which might be taken from them. These [persons] are not poor in spirit because a person who is truly poor in spirit hates himself (cf. Luke 14:26) and loves those who strike him on the cheek (cf. Matt. 5:39).

—St. Francis, The Admonitions, XIV

Humility is the recognition of the truth about God and ourselves.

—St. Francis

I caution the friars and beg them not to look down upon or pass judgment on those people whom they see wearing soft and colorful clothing and enjoying the choicest food and drink. Instead, each must criticize and despise himself.

—St. Francis, Final Rule of the Friars Minor 1223, II

Blessed is that servant (cf. Matt. 24:46) who does not pride himself on the good that the Lord says or does through him any more than on what He says or does through another. That person sins who wishes to receive more from his neighbor than what he is willing to give of himself to the Lord God.

—St. Francis, The Admonitions, XVII

Blessed is the servant who would accept correction, accusation, and blame from another as patiently as he would from himself. Blessed is the servant who when he is rebuked quietly agrees, respectfully submits, humbly admits his fault, and willingly makes amends. Blessed is the servant who is not quick to excuse himself and who humbly accepts shame and blame for a sin, even though he did not commit any fault.

—St. Francis, The Admonitions, XXIII

Poverty, Humility, Charity, and Obedience

Blessed is the person who bears with his neighbor in his
weakness to the degree that he would wish to be sustained by
him if he were in a similar situation (cf. Gal. 6:2; Matt. 7:12).

—St. Francis, The Admonitions, XVIII

Blessed is that servant who stores up in heaven (cf. Matt. 6:20)
the good things which the Lord has revealed to him and does
not desire to reveal them to others in the hope of profiting
thereby, for the Most High Himself will manifest His deeds
to whomever He wishes. Blessed is the servant who keeps the
secrets of the Lord in his heart.

—St. Francis, The Admonitions, XXVIII

And as they went on their way conversing, according to their
custom, of God, the friar (remembering his vision) bethought
him to ask the man of God what he thought of himself. To which
Christ's humble servant made reply: "I think myself to be the
greatest of sinners." And when the brother answered that he could
not with a safe conscience say or think such a thing, he added: "If
Christ had shown to the most wicked man on earth such mercy as
He has shown to me, I believe assuredly that that man would have
been far more grateful to God than I have been."

—St. Francis, *The Life of St. Francis of Assisi* by St. Bonaventure

Brother Francis, the least of your servants, worthless and sinful, sends greetings.

—St. Francis

In icons of God and the Virgin Mary they are honored and remembered, yet the paint and the panels ascribe nothing to themselves because they are just pigment and boards.

—St. Francis preaches about the humility he expects of his brothers, from *The Legend of Perugia*

No man ought wickedly to pride himself upon such things as a sinner can do. A sinner can fast, pray, weep, mortify his flesh; this only he cannot do—be faithful to his Lord. In this, then, we may glory—if we give Him the glory which is due to Him, if we serve Him faithfully, if we ascribe all His gifts to Him.

—St. Francis, *The Life of St. Francis of Assisi* by St. Bonaventure

Poverty, Humility, Charity, and Obedience

Blessed is the servant who esteems himself no better when he is praised and exalted by people than when he is considered worthless, simple, and despicable; for what a man is before God, that he is and nothing more. Woe to that religious who has been placed in a high position by others and does not wish to come down of his own will. *And blessed is that servant* (cf. Matt. 24:46) who does not place himself in a high position of his own will and always desires to be under the feet of others.

—St. Francis, The Admonitions, XX

Blessed is the servant who is found to be as humble among his subjects as he would be among his masters. Blessed is the servant who remains always under the rod of correction. He is *the faithful and prudent servant* (cf. Matt. 24:45) who for all his offenses does not delay in punishing himself, inwardly through contrition and outwardly through confession and penance for what he did.

—St. Francis, The Admonitions, XXIV

He studied to conceal the gifts of the Lord in the secret of his breast, lest, turning to his glory, they might become the occasion of his ruin. When he heard himself praised and blessed by many, he would often say: "I may yet have sons and daughters; you cannot safely praise me. No man is to be praised whose end is uncertain."

—*The Life of St. Francis* by St. Bonaventure

It would be considered a theft on our part if we didn't give to someone in greater need than we are.

—St. Francis

Let us then have charity and humility; let us give alms since this washes our souls from the stains of [our] sins (cf. Tob. 4:11; 12:9). For people lose everything they leave behind in this world; but they carry with them the rewards of charity and the alms which they gave, for which they will have a reward and a suitable remuneration from the Lord.

—St. Francis, Letter to All the Faithful, Second Version

They should offer no resistance to injury (cf. Matt. 5:39); indeed, if someone slaps them on one cheek, they should offer him the other as well (cf. Matt. 5:39; Luke 6: 29). And if one takes their cloak, let them not hang on to their tunic. Let them give to everyone who begs from them; and if some one carries off things that belong to them, they should not demand them back (cf. Luke 6:30).

—St. Francis, Rule of 1221, XIV

For, dear brother, courtesy is one of the qualities of God,
who courteously gives His sun and His rain and everything
to the just and to the unjust. And courtesy is a sister of charity.
It extinguishes hatred and keeps love alive.

—St. Francis, from *The Little Flowers of St. Francis*

Everything people leave after them in this world is lost, but for
their charity and almsgiving they will receive a reward from God.

—St. Francis

But as for me, I desire this privilege from the Lord, that never
may I have any privilege from man, except to do reverence to
all, and to convert the world by obedience to the Holy Rule
rather by example than by word.

—St. Francis, from *The Little Flowers of Saint Francis*

We ought also to deny ourselves and to put our bodies beneath
the yoke of servitude and holy obedience as each one has
promised to the Lord. And let no man be bound by obedience
to obey any one in that where sin or offence is committed.

—St. Francis, Letter to All the Faithful

The Lord says in the Gospel: *He who does not renounce everything he possesses cannot be my disciple* (cf. Luke 14:33); and: *He who wishes to save his life must lose it* (cf. Luke 9:24). That person leaves everything he possesses and loses his body who surrenders his whole self to obedience at the hands of his prelate.[1] And whatever he does and says which he knows is not contrary to his [prelate's] will, provided that what he does is good, is true obedience. And should the subject sometimes see that some things might be better and more useful for his soul than what the prelate may command him, let him willingly offer such things to God as a sacrifice; and instead earnestly try to fulfill the wishes of the prelate. For this is loving obedience because it pleases God and neighbor.

—St. Francis, The Admonitions, III

I speak to you, as I can, concerning the state of our soul. You should accept as a grace all those things which deter you from loving the Lord God and whoever has become an impediment to you, whether [they are] brothers or others, even if they lay hands on you. And you should desire that things be this way and not otherwise. And let this be [an expression] of true obedience to the Lord God and to me, for I know full well that this is true obedience. And love those who do these things to you. And do not expect anything different from them, unless it is something which the Lord shall have given to you. And love them in this and do not wish that they be better Christians. And let this be more [valuable] to you than a hermitage.

—St. Francis, A Letter to a Minister

He is sitting with his companions, and he says something like

[1] *Prelate comes from the Latin word praelatus and is often used by Saint Francis when speaking about a friar who is a "superior."*

this: "There is hardly a friar in the whole world who obeys perfectly." Taken aback, his brothers say to him: "Tell us, Father, what is the perfect and highest obedience." And Francis replies, using the figure of a corpse to describe the truly obedient person. "Take a corpse and place it wherever you want. You will see that it doesn't resist being moved, it doesn't complain about its position, it doesn't cry out if it is allowed to lie there. If it is placed on a chair, it won't look up but down; if it is clothed in purple, it looks twice as pale. This is true obedience: not to ask why you are moved, not to care where you are placed, not to insist on being changed somewhere else. Raised to an office, you retain your accustomed humility; the more you are honored, the more unworthy you consider yourself."

—*The Way of St. Francis* by Murray Bodo

Amongst many gifts which our Lord in His goodness has bestowed upon me, He has granted me this grace—to obey with the same readiness a novice who had been but an hour in religion, were he set over me as my superior, as the most ancient and discreet amongst the brethren.

—St. Francis, *The Life of St. Francis of Assisi* by St. Bonaventure

Hail, Queen Wisdom, may the Lord protect you
    with your sister, holy pure Simplicity.
Lady, holy Poverty, may the Lord protect you
    with your sister, holy Humility.
Lady, holy Charity, may the Lord protect you
    with your sister, holy Obedience..
O most holy Virtues, may the Lord protect all of you,
    from Whom you come and proceed.
There is surely no one in the entire world
    who can possess any one of you
    unless he dies first.
Whoever possesses one [of you]
    and does not offend the others,
    possesses all.
And whoever offends one [of you]
    does not possess any
    and offends all.
And each one destroys vices and sins.
Holy Wisdom destroys
Satan and all his subtlety.
Pure holy Simplicity destroys
    all the wisdom of this world
    and the wisdom of the body.
Holy Poverty destroys
    the desires of riches
    and avarice
    and the cares of this world.
Holy Humility destroys
    pride
    and all the people who are in the world
    and all things that belong to the world.

Holy Charity destroys
    every temptation of the devil and of the flesh
    and every carnal fear.
Holy Obedience destroys
    every wish of the body and of the flesh
    and binds its mortified body
    to obedience of the Spirit
    and to obedience of one's brother
    and [the person who possesses her] is subject and submissive
    to all persons in the world
    and not to man only
    but even to all beasts and wild animals
    so that they may do whatever they want with him
    inasmuch as it has been given to them from above
    by the Lord.

  —St. Francis, The Salutation of the Virtues

Where there is charity and wisdom
    there is neither fear nor ignorance.
Where there is patience and humility,
    there is neither anger nor disturbance.
Where there is poverty with joy,
    there is neither covetousness nor avarice.
Where there is inner peace and meditation,
    there is neither anxiousness nor dissipation.
Where there is fear of the Lord to guard the house
    (cf. Luke 11:21),
    there the enemy cannot gain entry.
Where there is mercy and discernment,
    there is neither excess nor hardness of heart.

—St. Francis, The Admonitions, XXVII

SUFFERING AND SACRIFICE

I hope that I so blessed shall be
That every suffering pleaseth me.

—St. Francis

Be patient, because the weaknesses of the body are given to us in this world by God for the salvation of soul. So they are of great merit when they are borne patiently.

—St. Francis, from *The Little Flowers of St. Francis*

And I ask the friar who is sick to give thanks to the Creator for all things; and to desire to be whatever the Lord wills him to be, whether well or sick, for all whom God has destined for life eternal (cf. Acts 13:48) He instructs by the rod of afflictions and infirmities and by the spirit of compunction, as the Lord says: "Those whom I love I correct and chastise" (cf. Apoc. 3:19).

—St. Francis, Rule of 1221, X

And we ought rather to rejoice when we would fall into every sort of trial (cf. James 1: 2), and would have to put up with all kinds of afflictions or tribulations of soul or body in this world for the sake of life eternal.

—St. Francis, Rule of 1221, XVII

Let each man glory in his own sufferings and not in another's.

—St. Francis, *The Chronicle of Jordan of Giano*

He began to exercise such severe discipline over all his sensual appetites, that he hardly took such food as was necessary for the support of nature. For he said that it was hard to satisfy the necessities of the body without indulging the inclinations of the senses. Therefore he rarely ate any food which had been cooked with fire; and when he did so, he mixed so much water therewith as to render it insipid. And what shall I say of his drinking?— for he would hardly allow himself cold water enough to slake the burning thirst with which he was oftentimes tormented. He continually discovered new ways of exercising abstinence, increasing daily in its exercise; and even when he had attained the summit of perfection he still endeavored, as if only a beginner, to punish, by fresh macerations, the rebellion of the flesh.

—*The Life of St. Francis of Assisi* by St. Bonaventure

Hence he called his body *Brother Ass,* saying that it was to be laden with heavy burdens, beaten with many stripes, and fed with poor and scanty food.

—*The Life of St. Francis of Assisi* by St. Bonaventure

Brother, It isn't good to refuse to have your eyes treated, for your health and your life are very valuable—to yourself and other people. You, who have always shown such sympathy for your brothers when they were ill shouldn't be so callous toward yourself, for your illness is serious and clearly needs treatment. That is why I command you to submit to it.

—Letter from Brother Elias urging St. Francis to seek medical treatment for his eyes, from *The Legend of Perugia*, quoted in *Francis of Assisi: A Revolutionary Life* by Adrian House

Oh, brother fire, the Most High has created thee glorious, mighty, beautiful, and useful above all other creatures. Be thou propitious and healthful to me at this hour. I beseech the great Lord, Who created thee, so sweetly to temper thy heat that I may be able to endure it.

—St. Francis prays before having his face cauterized with a hot iron to cure his eye problems. The hot iron, miraculously, did not cause him any pain. From *The Life of St. Francis of Assisi* by St. Bonaventure

Once when Francis was very ill, he was so weak that he could not even move. But when one of the brothers asked what he would prefer to bear, this lingering, protracted illness or the suffering of an excruciating martyrdom at the hands of an executioner, he replied, "My son, what has always been and still is most dear to me and sweeter and more acceptable is whatever the Lord my God is most pleased to let happen in me and to me, for my only desire is to be found always conformed and obedient to his will in everything. Yet, if you need to know, this infirmity is harder for me to bear even for three days than any martyrdom. I am not speaking of the reward, of course, but of the intensity of suffering it causes."

—*The Way of St. Francis* by Murray Bodo

And because I see that I am drawing near to death, I intend to stay alone and recollect myself with God and weep over my sins before Him. And let Brother Leo, whenever it seems right to him, bring me a little bread and a little water. And on no account let any lay persons come to me, but deal with them yourselves.

—St. Francis to his brothers before retiring to Alvernia, from *The Little Flowers of St. Francis*

O Lord, I beg of you two graces before I die—to experience personally and in all possible fullness the pains of your bitter Passion, and to feel for you the same love that moved you to sacrifice yourself for us.

—St. Francis's prayer at Alvernia, where he received the stigmata, from *The Little Flowers of St. Francis*

One morning two years before his death, about the feast of the Exaltation of the Cross, while he was praying on the side of a mountain named Alvernia, there appeared to him a seraph in the beautiful figure of a crucified man, having his hands and feet extended as though on a cross, and clearly showing the face of Jesus Christ. Two wings met above his head, two covered the rest of his body to the feet, and two were spread as in flight. When the vision passed, the soul of Francis was afire with love; and on his body there appeared the wonderful impression of the wounds of our Lord Jesus Christ.

—*The Legend of the Three Companions*

He hid these marks from strangers most assiduously, and concealed them with the utmost care from those close to him, so that even the friars nearest to him, his most devoted followers, long remained ignorant of them.

—*The First Life of St. Francis* by Thomas of Celano

But divine providence did not want them always hidden, unrevealed to those dear to him. And the very fact that his limbs were exposed did not permit their concealment. But when once one of his companions saw the stigmata in his feet, he said to him: "Good brother, what is this?" And he replied: "Mind your own business." Another time, a brother took his tunic to wash it, and seeing the bloodstains said to the Blessed when he gave it back to him: "What was that blood spotting your tunic?" And putting his fingers to his eye, the Blessed said: "Knowing that this is an eye, do you ask what it is?" . . . When anyone asked for his hand to kiss, he would give only enough of his fingers for a kiss to be possible and sometimes offered only his sleeve. He wrapped his feet in woolen footcloths, so that they would not be seen, putting skins over the wool to lessen the pain of it. And although it was impossible for the holy father to hide the stigmata in his hands and feet completely from his companions, if anyone did see them, he was nonetheless bitter about it.

—*The Second Life of St. Francis* by Thomas of Celano

Being forced by necessity, he chose Brother Leo, who was simpler and purer than the others. And he revealed everything to him, and he let him see and touch those holy wounds. And St. Francis entrusted his wounds only to him to be touched and rebound with new bandages between those marvelous nails and the remaining flesh, to relieve the pain and absorb the blood which issued and flowed from the wounds.

—*The Little Flowers of St. Francis*

What I had been fearing has overtaken me and you . . . the man who used to carry us like lambs on his shoulders has set out for a far country . . . we are fatherless orphans . . . . But now I have told you that, I must announce a great joy to you, a new miracle: a sign unheard of since time began, except in the Lord Christ, the Son of God. A short time before his death, our Brother and Father was seen to be like the Crucified, having in his body the five wounds that are Christ's marks. His hands and feet bore the scars of nails, being pierced on each side, carrying the marks and color of nails. His side looked as though it had been laid open with a lance, and bled frequently.

> —Letter from Brother Elias, Minister General of the Order to Brother Gregory, minister of friars in France written on the day of St. Francis's death, October 3, 1226

My Lord Jesus Christ, I thank You for the great love and charity which You are showing me, because it is a sign of great love when the Lord punishes His servant well for all his faults in this world, so that he may not be punished for them in the next world. And I am prepared to endure with joy every pain and every adversity which You, my God, wish to send me for my sins.

> —St. Francis, from *The Little Flowers of St. Francis*

Suffering and Sacrifice

The highest gift and grace of the Holy Spirit that Christ concedes to His friends is to conquer oneself and, out of love of Christ, to endure willingly sufferings, injuries, insults, and discomfort. We cannot glory in all the other gifts of God because they are not ours but they are of God, because of which the Apostle says, "What do you have that does not come from God? If you have had it from God, why do you glory in it as if it were your own?"

—St. Francis

You damned spirits! You can only do what the hand of God allows you to do. Therefore in the name of Almighty God I tell you to do whatever God allows you to do to my body. I will gladly endure it since I have no worse enemy than my body. If you take revenge on my enemy for me, you do me a very great favor.

—St. Francis

One Lent he was whittling a little cup to occupy his spare moments and to prevent them from being wasted. When he was reciting Terce, it came into his mind and distracted him a little. Moved by fervor of spirit, he burned the cup in the fire, saying: "I will sacrifice this to the Lord, whose sacrifice it has impeded."

—*The Life of St. Francis of Assisi* by St. Bonaventure

Even if you were more handsome and richer than everyone else and even if you performed wonders such as driving out demons, all these things would be an obstacle to you and none of them would belong to you nor could you glory in any of these things. But in this we can glory: in our infirmities (cf. 2 Cor. 12:5) and bearing daily the holy cross of our Lord Jesus Christ (cf. Luke 14:27)

—St. Francis, The Admonitions, V

We must also fast and abstain from vices and sins (cf. Sir 3:32) and from any excess of food and drink, and be Catholics. We must also visit churches frequently and venerate and show respect for the clergy, not so much for them personally if they are sinners, but by reason of their office and their administration of the most holy Body and Blood of Christ which they sacrifice upon the altar and receive and administer to others. And let all of us firmly realize that no one can be saved except through the holy words and Blood of our Lord Jesus Christ which the clergy pronounce, proclaim and minister.

—St. Francis, Letter to All the Faithful, Second Version

Our friends, then, are all those who unjustly afflict upon us trials and ordeals, shame and injustice, sorrows and torments, martyrdom and death; we must love them greatly for we will possess eternal life because of what they bring upon us.

—St. Francis

TEMPTATION, SIN, AND FORGIVENESS

May God bless you and protect you from all temptations! Do not be troubled because you have temptations. For I consider you more of a servant and friend of God and I love you more, the more you are attacked by temptations. Truly I tell you that no one should consider himself a perfect friend of God until he has passed through many temptations and tribulations.

—St. Francis to Brother Leo, from *The Little Flowers of St. Francis*

Go, my son, and confess, and do not abandon your habit of prayer. Know in all certainty that this temptation will be of great usefulness and consolation, and you will soon have a proof thereof.

—St. Francis

I have been all things unholy. If God can work through me, He can work through anyone.

—St. Francis

Sinners are led back to God by holy meekness better than by cruel scolding.

—St. Francis, reprimanding Brother Angelo for driving away three robbers who came begging for food, from *The Little Flowers of St. Francis*

TEMPTATION, SIN, AND FORGIVENESS

See, blind ones, deceived by your enemies: by the flesh, the world, and the devil; since it is sweet to the body to commit sin and it is bitter for it to serve God; since all vices and sins come forth and proceed from the heart of man, just as the Lord says in the Gospel (cf. Mark 7:21). And you will have nothing in this age nor in the one to come. And you think you will possess the vanities of this age for a long time, but you are deceived, since there will come the day and hour, of which you do not think, know or pay attention; the body weakens, death approaches and this man dies a bitter death. And wheresoever, whensoever, howsoever a man dies in culpable sin without penance and satisfaction, if he can make satisfaction and does not, the devil tears his soul from his body with such anguish and tribulation, that no one can know it, except him who experiences it. And all talents and power and knowledge and wisdom (2 Chron. 1:12), which they thought they had, and he bears it way from them (cf. Luke 8:18; Mark 4:25).

—St. Francis, Letter to All the Faithful

Many people, when they sin or receive an injury, often blame the enemy or some neighbor. But this is not right, for each one has the [real] enemy in his own power; that is, the body through which he sins. *Therefore blessed is that servant* (cf. Matt. 24:46) who, having such an enemy in his power, will always hold him captive and wisely guard himself against him, because as long as he does this, no other enemy, seen or unseen, will be able to harm him.

—St. Francis, The Admonitions, X

I confess all my sins to the Lord God, the Father and the Son and the Holy Spirit, to the Blessed Mary ever Virgin, and to all the saints in heaven and on earth, to Brother H., the Minister of our Order, as to my venerable Lord, and to the priests of our Order and to all my other blessed brothers. I have offended [God] in many ways through my grievous fault especially in not having kept the Rule which I promised the Lord nor in having said the Office as the Rule prescribes, either out of negligence or on account of my sickness, or because I am ignorant and unlearned. Therefore, through every means which I am capable of employing, I ask Brother H., the Minister General [and] my lord, to insist that the Rule be observed inviolably by everyone. [Further, he should insist] that the clerics say the Office with devotion before God, not concentrating on the melody of the voice but on the harmony of the mind, so that the voice may blend with the mind, and the mind be in harmony with God.

—St. Francis, Letter to the Entire Order

Nothing should upset the servant of God except sin. And no matter how another person may sin, if the servant of God lets himself become angry and disturbed because of this, [and] not because of love, he stores up the guilt for himself. (cf. Rom. 2:5). That servant of God who does not become angry or upset at anything lives justly and without anything of his own. And he is blessed who does not keep anything for himself, rendering to Caesar what is Caesar's, and to God what is God's (cf. Matt. 22:21).

—St. Francis, The Admonitions, XI

Temptation, Sin, and Forgiveness

Whoever envies his brother the good which the Lord says or does in him commits a sin of blasphemy, because he envies the Most High Who says and does every good.

—St. Francis, The Admonitions, VIII

I strictly command all the friars not to have any associations or meetings with women which could arouse suspicion. Moreover, with the exception of those granted special permission by the Apostolic See, they are not to enter the monasteries of nuns. Again, to avoid what might provoke scandal either among the friars or about them, they are not to act as godfathers for men or women.

—St. Francis, Final Rule of the Friars Minor 1223, XI

Should any friars succumb to the temptations of the enemy and fall grievously into such sins as may have been reserved among the friars to the ministers provincial, then such friars must betake themselves to the ministers as soon as possible, without delay. If the ministers are priests, they are with mercy to impose a penance upon them. If they are not priests, they should have such a penance imposed by some priest of the Order as may seem to them most advisable according to the will of God. They must take care likewise not to be angered or disturbed because of the sin which another may commit, since anger and anxiety hinder charity in themselves and in the sinners.

—St. Francis, Final Rule of the Friars Minor 1223, VII

There should not be any brother in the world who has sinned, however much he may have possibly sinned, who, after he has looked into your eyes, would go away without having received your mercy, if he is looking for mercy. And if he were not to seek mercy, you should ask him if he wants mercy. And if he should sin thereafter a thousand times before your very eyes, love him more than me so that you may draw him back to the Lord. Always be merciful to [brothers] such as these.

—St. Francis, A Letter to a Minister

HUMAN NATURE

In the loss of dignity, in the absence of praise, in humble subjection, there is great profit to the soul. Why, therefore, when time has been given us to profit withal, do we seek rather for peril than for profit?

—St. Francis, *The Life of St. Francis of Assisi* by St. Bonaventure

Let all of us brothers guard against all pride and vainglory, and keep ourselves from the wisdom of this world and the prudence of the flesh (cf. Rom. 8:6). For the prompting of the flesh seeks and strives to be full of talk, but cares little for action; and seeks not God-centeredness and holiness in the inner man, but looks for and desires a religiosity and holiness that can be seen by men. And it is of these that the Lord says: "Amen, I say to you, they have received their reward" (cf. Matt. 6:2). The Spirit of the Lord, on the other hand, wishes the outer man to be mortified and despised and considered mean and of little worth; and strives instead for humility and patience and for the pure and simple and true peace of the inner man.

—St. Francis, Rule of 1221, XVII

I warn the friars and implore them in the Lord Jesus Christ, that they keep themselves from all pride, vainglory, envy, avarice, the cares and worries of this world, detraction and complaint. And those who have no book-learning should not set their heart on acquiring it. Instead, let them pursue what above all else they must desire: to have the spirit of the Lord and the workings of His grace, to pray always to Him with a clean heart, and to have humility, patience in persecution and weakness, and to love those who persecute us or rebuke us; for the Lord says: "Love your enemies, and pray for those who persecute and calumniate you" (cf. Matt. 5:44). "Blessed are they who suffer persecution for justice' sake: for theirs is the kingdom of heaven" (cf. Matt. 5:10). "He that shall persevere to the end, he shall be saved" (cf. Matt. 10:22).

—St. Francis, Final Rule of the Friars Minor 1223, X

Brother Body is our cell, and our soul is a hermit who stays within it praying to the Lord and meditating on Him.

—St. Francis, from *The Legend of the Three Companions*

Be conscious, O man, of the wondrous state in which the Lord God has placed you, for He created you and formed you to the image of His beloved Son according to the body, and to His likeness according to the spirit (cf. Gen. 1:26). And yet all the creatures under heaven each according to its nature serve, know, and obey their Creator better than you. And even the demons did not crucify him, but you together with them have crucified Him and crucify Him even now by delighting in vices and sins.

—St. Francis, The Admonitions, V

We must hate our bodies with [their] vices and sins, because the Lord says in the Gospel: All evils, vices, and sins proceed from the heart (cf. Matt. 15:18-19; Mark 7:23).

—St. Francis, Letter to All the Faithful, Second Version

Blessed is that religious who takes no pleasure and joy except in the most holy words and deeds of the Lord and with these leads people to the love of God in joy and gladness. Woe to that religious who delights in idle and frivolous words and with these provokes people to laughter.

—St. Francis, The Admonitions, XX

When the soul is troubled, lonely, and darkened, then it turns easily to the outer comfort and to the empty enjoyments of the world.

—St. Francis

KNOWLEDGE

A nd he who would attain to this height of perfection
must lay aside not only worldly prudence, but even all
knowledge of letters; that thus, stripped of all things, he may
come to see what is the power of the Lord, and cast himself
naked into the arms of the Crucified.

—St. Francis, on poverty as the means of salvation, from
The Life of St. Francis of Assisi by St. Bonaventure

And we were without learning, and subject to all. And I was
wont to work with my hands, and I still wish to do so. And I
earnestly wish that all the friars be occupied with some kind
of work, as long as it becomes our calling. Those who do not
know how [to work] should learn, not indeed out of any desire
to receive the pay which the work may bring, but to give a good
example and to avoid idleness.

—*Testament of the Holy Father St. Francis*

The Apostle says: "The letter kills, but the spirit gives life" (cf. 2 Cor 3:6). Those are killed by the letter who merely wish to know the words alone, so that they may be esteemed as wiser than others and be able to acquire great riches to give to [their] relatives and friends. In a similar way, those religious are killed by the letter who do not wish to follow the spirit of Sacred Scripture, but only wish to know [what] the words [are] and [how to] interpret them to others. And those are given life by the spirit of Sacred Scripture who do not refer to themselves any text which they know or seek to know, but, by word and example, return everything to the most high Lord God to Whom every good belongs.

—St. Francis, The Admonitions, VII

I am pleased for my friars to study the Scriptures as long as they do not neglect application to prayer, after the example of Christ, of whom we read that he prayed more than he read.

—St. Francis, *The Life of St. Francis of Assisi* by St. Bonaventure

And all theologians and those who impart the holy words of God, we must honor and reverence as those who minister to us spirit and life.

—*Testament of the Holy Father St. Francis*

KNOWLEDGE

Brother Leo, Little Lamb of God, even if a Friar Minor could speak with the voice of an angel, and knew the courses of the stars and the powers of herbs, and knew all about the treasures in the earth, and if he knew the qualities of birds and fishes, animals, humans, roots, trees, rocks, and waters, write down and note carefully that true joy is not in that.

—St. Francis, from *The Little Flowers of St. Francis*

Man has as much knowledge as he puts to work.

—St. Francis, from *The Mirror of Perfection*, early Franciscan work written by Brother Leo

The Lord said to Adam: "Eat of every tree; do not eat of the tree of knowledge of good and evil." He was able to eat of every tree of paradise since he did not sin as long as he did not go against obedience. For the person eats of the tree of the knowledge of good who appropriates to himself his own will and thus exalts himself over the good things which the Lord says and does in him; and thus, through the suggestions of the devil and the transgression of the command, what he eats becomes for him the fruit of the knowledge of evil. Therefore, it is necessary that he bear the punishment.

—St. Francis, The Admonitions, II

My brothers who are being led by their curious passion for learning will find their hand empty on the day of retribution when books, no longer useful, will be thrown out of windows and into cubbyholes.

—St. Francis, from *The Second Life of St. Francis* by Thomas of Celano

THE CHURCH

All the brothers are to be Catholics and live and speak in keeping with their belief. Should any one of them, however, have erred from the faith and the Catholic way of life in word or in deed and has not amended, he is to be altogether expelled from our brotherhood. And we are to regard all clerics and all religious as masters in the things that regard the salvation of souls and do not deviate from our religion; and we are to hold in reverence their order and office and administration in the Lord.

—St. Francis, Rule 1221, XIX

The Lord gave me and still gives me such faith in priests who live according to the manner of the holy Roman Church because of their order, that if they were to persecute me, I would still have recourse to them. And if I possessed as much wisdom as Solomon had and I came upon pitiful priests of this world, I would not preach contrary to their will in the parishes in which they live. And I desire to fear, love, and honor them and all others as my masters.

—*Testament of the Holy Father St. Francis*

We have been sent to help the clergy, to supply whatever is lacking in them. . . . Winning souls is what pleases God most and we can do this better by working with the clergy than against them. If they obstruct people's salvation retribution belongs to God, and He will punish them in His own time. So obey your superiors and let there be no jealousy on your part. If you are sons of peace you will win both clergy and people. . . . Conceal their mistakes and make up for their many defects; and when you have done this be more humble than before.

—St. Francis, *The Legend of Perugia* quoted in *Francis of Assisi: A Revolutionary Life* by Adrian House

THE CHURCH

Blessed is the servant who has faith in the clergy who live uprightly according to the norms of the Roman Church. And woe to those who look down upon them; for even though they may be sinners, nonetheless no one is to judge them since the Lord alone reserves judgment on them to Himself. For inasmuch as their ministry is greater in that it concerns the most holy Body and Blood of our Lord Jesus Christ, which they receive and which they alone administer to others, so those who sin against them commit a greater sin than [if they sinned] against all other people of this world.

—St. Francis, The Admonitions, XXVI

Listen my brothers: if the blessed Virgin is so honored, as it is right, since she carried Him in her most holy womb; if the blessed Baptist trembled and did not dare to touch the holy head of God; if the tomb in which He lay for some time is so venerated, how holy, just, and worthy must be the person who touches Him with his hands, receives Him in his heart and mouth, and offers Him to others to be received.

—St. Francis

No Brother is to preach in a manner contrary to the laws of the Church or without the permission of his minister.

—St. Francis, Rule of 1221, XVII

I charge the ministers by obedience to ask of the Lord Pope one of the cardinals of the Holy Roman Church, to be ruler, protector and corrector of the brotherhood, to this end: that always submitted to the same Holy Church, prostrate at her feet, and firm in the Catholic faith, we may observe the poverty and humility and the Holy Gospel of our Lord Jesus Christ, as we have firmly promised.

—St. Francis, Final Rule of the Friars Minor 1223, XII

Prayers and Blessings
of Saint Francis

M ost high,
glorious God,
    enlighten the darkness of my heart
    and give me, Lord,
    a correct faith,
    a certain hope,
    a perfect charity,
    sense and knowledge,
    so that I may carry our Your holy and true command.

—The first recorded prayer of St. Francis, dating back to
   when he was about twenty-three years old and struggling
   to discern his vocation

Lord, make me an instrument of Your peace.
Where there is hatred, let me sow love;
Where there is injury, pardon;
Where there is friction, union;
Where there is error, truth;
Where there is doubt, faith;
Where there is despair, hope;
Where there is darkness, light;
Where there is sadness, joy.

O Divine Master,
Grant that I may not so much seek
    to be consoled as to console,
    to be understood as to understand,
    to be loved as to love,

For it is in giving that we receive.
It is in pardoning that we are pardoned.
It is in dying that we are born to eternal life.

  —The Prayer of St. Francis, recited the world over in his name,
    was probably written in France about 1912

Almighty, eternal, just and merciful God,
grant us in our misery [the grace]
 to do for You alone
 what we know You want us to do
 and always
 to desire what pleases You.
Thus,
 inwardly cleansed,
 interiorly enlightened,
 and inflamed by the fire of the Holy Spirit,
 may we be able to follow
 in the footprints of Your beloved Son,
 our Lord Jesus Christ.
And,
 by Your grace alone,
 may we make our way to You,
Most High,
Who live and rule
 in perfect Trinity and simple Unity,
 and are glorified,
God all-powerful,
 forever and ever.
Amen.

 —St. Francis, Letter to the Entire Order

You are holy,
O my Lord and only God,
    mysterious and holy,
    holy and amazing!

You are mighty, magnificent, transcendent.
You are all-powerful,
O most holy Creator,
    beneficent ruler of heaven and earth.

You are manifold and One at the same time,
Lord God.
You are utterly wonderful.
You are wonderful, perfectly wonderful,
    the very essence of all that is most wonderful,
O Lord God!
You are real and alive.

You are generosity and wisdom,
    humility and patience,
    safety and serenity,
    ecstasy and delight.

You are righteousness and balance,
    prosperity that surpasses all basic needs,
    you are harmony and beauty.

You are my protector, guardian, and defender.
You are my strength.
You are my sustenance and courage.

You are faith, hope, and charity.
You are my deepest tenderness.
You are everlasting vitality.

O supreme and marvelous Lord,
Almighty God,
Beloved redeemer,
You are absolute mercy.

   —St. Francis, The Praises of God

May the fiery and honey-sweet power
    of your love, O Lord,
Wean me from all things under heaven,
    so that I may die
    for love of your love,
You who were so good as to die
    for love of my love.

   —Prayer attributed to St. Francis by St. Bernardino

Let the whole of mankind tremble
    the whole world shake
    and the heavens exult
    when Christ, the Son of the living God,
    is [present] on the altar
    in the hands of a priest.
O admirable heights and sublime lowliness!
O sublime humility!
O humble sublimity!
That the Lord of the universe,
    God and the Son of God,
    so humbles Himself
    that for our salvation
He hides Himself under the little form of bread!
Look, brothers, at the humility of God
    and pour out your hearts before Him!
Humble yourselves, as well,
    that you may be exalted by Him.
Therefore,
    hold back nothing of yourselves for yourselves
    so that
He Who gives Himself totally to you
    may receive you totally.

   —St. Francis, Letter to the Entire Order

Hail, O Lady, Holy Queen, God's Holy Mother Mary!
You have been made the Virgin Church
And chosen by the most Holy Father in heaven.
You has He consecrated with His most holy beloved Son
    and the Holy Spirit the Paraclete
In You there has been, and is,
    all fullness of Grace, and all that is good.
Hail His Palace! His Tabernacle!
Hail His Dwelling Place!
Hail His Garment! His Handmaid!
Hail His Mother!
And (hail) all you holy Virtues [in her] which by the grace and
    enlightenment of the Holy Spirit
    are poured forth into the hearts of the faithful,
    that from faithless souls
You [virtues] may make them faithful to God!

  —St. Francis, The Salutation to Our Lady

May God bless and keep you,
May God smile upon you, and have mercy upon you.
May God turn his face towards you,
And give you peace
May God bless, Leo, you.

  —St. Francis, Blessing to Brother Leo

Write this just as I tell you: Brother Bernard was the first brother whom the Lord gave me, as well as the first to put into practice and fulfill most completely the perfection of the Holy Gospel by distributing all his goods to the poor; because of this and many other prerogatives, I am bound to love him more than any other brother of the entire Order. Therefore, as much as I can, I desire and command that, whoever the minister general is, he should cherish and honor him as he would me, and likewise the ministers provincial and the brothers of the entire Order should esteem him in place of me.

> —St. Francis's blessing to Brother Bernard of Quintavalle, from *The Legend of Perugia* and quoted in *Francis and Clare: The Complete Works* edited by Regis J. Armstrong and Ignatius C. Brady

To console her [St. Francis] sent her in writing his blessing and likewise absolved her from any failure if she had committed any against his orders and wishes and the commands and wishes of the Son of God.

> —St. Francis dictated a blessing to St. Clare, sent to her during his last week of life, as she was sick and afraid of dying without hearing from him, from *The Legend of Perugia* and quoted in *Francis and Clare: The Complete Works* edited by Regis J. Armstrong and Ignatius C. Brady

PRAYERS AND BLESSINGS OF SAINT FRANCIS

Let us be ashamed to be caught up by worthless imaginings, for at the time of prayer we speak to the great King.

—St. Francis, *The Second Life* by Thomas of Celano

THE NATURAL WORLD

All creatures have the same source as we have. Like us, they derive the life of thought, love, and will from the Creator. Not to hurt our humble brethren is our first duty to them; but to stop there is a complete misapprehension of the intentions of Providence. We have a higher mission. God wishes that we should succor them whenever they require it.

—St. Francis

At dawn, when the sun rises, we should praise God, who created Brother Sun for us, and through him gives light to our eyes by day. And at nightfall everyone should praise God for Brother Fire, by whom He gives light to our eyes in the darkness. For we are all blind, and by these two brothers of ours God gives light to our eyes, so we should give special praise to our Creator for these and other creatures that serve us day by day.

—St. Francis, from *The Mirror of Perfection*

The Natural World

These creatures minister to our needs every day: without them we could not live; and through them the human race greatly offends the Creator. Every day, we fail to appreciate so great a blessing by not praising as we should the Creator and Dispenser of all these gifts.

—St. Francis

My sister birds, you owe much to God, and you must always and in every place give praise to Him; for He has given you freedom to wing through the sky and He has clothed you . . . You neither sow nor reap and God feeds you and gives you rivers and fountains for your thirst, and mountains and valleys for shelter, and tall trees for your nests. And although you neither know how to spin nor weave, God dresses you and your children, for the Creator loves you greatly and He blesses you abundantly. Therefore, my little bird sister, be careful not to be ungrateful, but strive always to praise God.

—St. Francis, from *The Little Flowers of St. Francis*

Though the Crow, black and frightening, is the antithesis of the dove, Francis's crow, thanks to his master, went to choir with the brothers, ate with them in the refectory, and visited the sick in the infirmary of the friary. He also went with them to Assisi's houses to beg for alms. When Francis died, the crow languished and would take no food. He refused to leave Francis's tomb and died there from grief and weakness.

—*The First Life of St. Francis* by Thomas of Celano

"Listen, dear people. Brother Wolf, who is standing here before you, has promised me and has given me a pledge that he will make peace with you and will never hurt you if you promise also to feed him every day. And I pledge myself as bondsman for Brother Wolf that he will faithfully keep this peace pact." . . . And the crowd was so filled with amazement and joy, out of devotion for the Saint as well as over the novelty of the miracle and over the peace pact between the wolf and the people, that they all shouted to the sky, praising and blessing the Lord Jesus Christ who had sent St. Francis to them, by whose merits they had been freed from such a fierce wolf and saved from such a terrible scourge and had recovered peace and quiet.

From that day, the wolf and the people kept the pact which St. Francis made. The wolf lived two years more, and it went from door to door for food. It hurt no one, and no one hurt it. The people fed it courteously. And it is a striking fact that not a single dog ever barked at it.

Then the wolf grew old and died. And the people were sorry, because whenever it went through the town, its peaceful kindness and patience reminded them of the virtues and the holiness of St. Francis.

—*The Little Flowers of St. Francis*

In the same lake was found a great fish, which was brought to him alive. After his custom, he called it by the name of brother, and put it back again into the water, near the boat in which he was. But the fish gamboled in the water before the man of God, and, as if attracted by the love of him, would by no means depart from the boat, until he sent it away with his blessing.

—*The Life of St. Francis of Assisi* by St. Bonaventure

Francis showed great tenderness for all of God's creatures, however humble. Remembering the Psalmist's words: As for me, I am a worm and no man. He would pick up any earth-worms he found in his path and carry them to safety, so that passers-by would not tread them underfoot.

—*The Wisdom of St. Francis and His Companions* by Stephen Clissold

One time when Francis was walking with another friar in the Venetian marshes, they came upon a huge flock of birds, singing among the reeds. When he saw them, the saint said to his companion, "Our sisters the birds are praising their Creator. We will go among them and sing God's praise, chanting the divine office." They went in among the birds, which remained where they were, making so much noise that the friars could not hear themselves saying the office. Eventually the saint turned to them and said, "My sisters, stop singing until we have given God the praise to which he has a right." The birds were immediately silent and remained that way until Francis gave them permission to sing again, after the men had taken plenty of time to say the office and had finished their praises. Then the birds began to sing again, as usual.

—*The Life of Saint Francis of Assisi* by St. Bonaventure

The beauty of the flowers brought him great delight of soul in their shape and color and sweet odor, and thus lifted his heart and soul to Him who is the Flower of Jesse. And when He came upon a field of flowers, He would preach to them as though they understood him and would invite them to praise the Lord. He often did the same in fields of grain, in vineyards, in the woods, the while he called on all things, earth and fire, air and wind, to love the Lord and serve Him!

—*The First Life of St. Francis* by Thomas of Celano

The Natural World

It would take too long and be well nigh impossible to gather together and recount all that the glorious Father Francis did and taught while he lived among men. For who could ever describe his great love whereby he was caught up in all things that belong to God? Who would be able to tell of the joy he felt as he contemplated in creatures the wisdom of the Creator, His power and His goodness? In very truth a marvelous and indescribable joy would often fill him when he beheld the sun and gazed at the moon, the stars, and the whole sweep of the heavens. Oh what simple piety and pious simplicity!

—*The First Life of St. Francis* by Thomas of Celano

Among the holy and admirable men who have revered nature as a wonderful gift of God to the human race, St. Francis of Assisi deserves special consideration. For he, in a special way, deeply sensed the universal works of the Creator and, filled with a certain divine spirit, sang that very beautiful "Canticle of the Creatures." Through them, Brother Sun most powerful and Sister Moon and the stars of heaven, he offered fitting praise, glory, honor and all blessing to the most high, all-powerful, good Lord. . . . Therefore, we proclaim St Francis of Assisi heavenly Patron of those who promote ecology.

—Apostolic Letter of Pope John Paul II, November 29, 1979

If you have men who will exclude any of God's creatures from the shelter of compassion and pity, you will have men who will deal likewise with their fellow men.

—St. Francis

God deigned to assure me, while I'm still here in the flesh, that there will be a place for me later in heaven. I therefore want to compose a song praising him and thanking him for all his creatures on earth, because we cannot live without them and we daily offend him by our lack of gratitude for them.

—St. Francis's words to his brothers about his composition of *The Canticle of Brother Sun,* from *The Legend of Perugia* and quoted in *Francis of Assisi: A Revolutionary Life* by Adrian House

The Canticle of Brother Sun

Most high, all-powerful, all good, Lord!
    All praise is yours, all glory, all honor
    And all blessing.

To you alone, Most High, do they belong.
    No mortal lips are worthy
    To pronounce your name.

All praise be yours, my Lord, through all that you have made,
    And first my lord Brother Sun,
    Who brings the day; and light you give to us through him.
How beautiful is he, how radiant in all his splendor!
    Of you, Most High, he bears the likeness.

All praise be yours, my Lord, through Sister Moon and Stars;
    In the heavens you have made them, bright
    And precious and fair.

All praise be yours, my Lord, through Brothers Wind and Air,
    And fair and stormy, all the weather's moods,
    By which you cherish all that you have made.

All praise be yours, my Lord, through Sister Water,
    So useful, lowly, precious and pure.
All praise be yours, my Lord, through Brother Fire,
    Through whom you brighten up the night.
    How beautiful he is, how gay! Full of power and strength.

All praise be yours, my Lord, through Sister Earth, our mother,
  Who feeds us in her sovereignty and produces
  Various fruits and colored flowers and herbs.

All praise be yours, my Lord, through those who grant pardon
  For love of you; through those who endure
  Sickness and trial.

Happy those who endure in peace,
  By you, Most High, they will be crowned.
All praise be yours, my Lord, through Sister Death,
  From whose embrace no mortal can escape.

Woe to those who die in mortal sin!
  Happy those she finds doing your will!
  The second death can do no harm to them.

Praise and bless my Lord, and give him thanks,
  And serve him with great humility.

REMEMBRANCES OF
SAINT FRANCIS

In the twelfth century, love burst onto the scene with extraordinary force, and Saint Francis was its champion.

—Hippolyte-Adolphe Taine

Francis sought occasion to love God in everything. In everything beautiful, he saw Him who is beauty itself.

—*The Life of St. Francis of Assisi* by St. Bonaventure

At the age of twenty-four Francis renounced both money and possessions. This, combined with his honesty, humility, and courage, released him from the burdens and restraints of worldly conventions and left him free to play God's troubadour and juggler. His song was love and he tossed up society's most cherished possessions—rank, wealth, fame, reputation, and power—exposing their flaws, so that their opposites seemed more precious than they.

—*Francis of Assisi: A Revolutionary Life* by Adrian House

Francis and his followers were comforted exceedingly in the absence of all things that are of this world.

—Thomas of Celano

The Franciscans spoke for the wretched of the earth, the men and women who during this violent epoch suffered unending injustice, ill-treatment, famine, epidemics, poverty, and the toll of recruitment for the quarrels of noblemen and the crusades of the church.

—*Alone of All Her Sex* by Marina Warner

Because they had nothing, they feared in no way to lose anything.

—Thomas of Celano

From humility, therefore, Francis desired that his friars should be called minors, and that the prelates of his Order should bear the name of minister, both to fulfill the words of the Gospel, which they had promised to observe, and also that his disciples might learn by the very name they bear that they have come to the school of the humble Jesus to learn humility.

—*The Life of St. Francis of Assisi* by St. Bonaventure

O how beautiful, how splendid, how glorious did he appear in the innocence of his life, in the simplicity of his words, in the purity of his heart, in his love for God, in his fraternal charity, in his ardent obedience, in his peaceful submission, in his angelic countenance!

—Thomas of Celano

Aroused by all things to the love of God,
    he rejoiced in all the works of the Lord's hands
    and from these joy-producing manifestations
    he rose to their life-giving
    principle and cause.
    In beautiful things
    he saw Beauty itself
    and through his vestiges imprinted on creation
    he followed his Beloved everywhere,
    making from all things a ladder
    by which he could climb up
    and embrace Him who is utterly desirable.

—*The Life of Saint Francis of Assisi* by St. Bonaventure

Francis's greatest concern was to be free from everything of this world, lest the serenity of his mind be disturbed even for an hour by the taint of anything that was mere dust.

—Thomas of Celano

Remembrances of Saint Francis

Saint Francis deprived himself of necessary things, which the brothers procured for him with great difficulty but most willingly; and after having cajoled us not to be angry, he gave away the great interior and external joy what he had denied his own body. That is why the minister general and his guardian forbade him to give his tunic to any brother without their permission. Some brothers, in fact, sometimes would ask him for it out of devotion, and he would immediately give it to them. It also sometimes happened that when he saw a sick or poorly clad brother, he would cut his habit in half and give him one part and keep the other for himself, for he had and wanted to have only one tunic.

—*The Legend of Perugia*

He would seek out some lonely spot or an abandoned church where he could go to pray at night.

—*The Life of St. Francis of Assisi* by St. Bonaventure

St. Francis had the custom of spending the whole day alone in his cell, and he did not come among the brothers unless the need for food forced him to come. But he did not come out to eat at fixed times, for a greater hunger for contemplation more often claimed him.

—*The Second Life of St. Francis* by Thomas of Celano

Here, in hidden secrecy, he defended himself before his Judge; here he pleaded with his Father; here he enjoyed the company of his divine Bridegroom; here he spoke with his Lover.

—*The Life of St. Francis of Assisi* by St. Bonaventure

Showered from his birth with favors from heaven,
filled with the spirit that inspired the prophets,
all aflame with the burning fire of the seraphim,
he is the one symbolized by the angel who rises
up from the East and bears the sign of the living God.

—St. Bonaventure

The saint had a horror of pride, which is the cause of all evil, and of disobedience, which is its worst offspring. On the other hand, he always had a warm welcome for humble repentance.

—St. Bonaventure

To him a man was always a man and did not disappear in a dense crowd any more than in a desert. He honored all men; that is, he not only loved but respected them all. What gave him his extraordinary personal power was this; that from the Pope to the beggar, from the sultan of Syria in his pavilion to the ragged robbers crawling out of the wood, there was never a man who looked into those brown burning eyes without being certain that Francis Bernardone was really interested in him; in his own inner individual life from the cradle to the grave; that he himself was being valued and taken seriously, and not merely added to the spoils of some social policy or the names in some clerical document.

—*St. Francis of Assisi* by G. K. Chesterton

When he stood in their midst to present his edifying words, he went completely blank and was unable to say anything at all. This he admitted with true humility and directed himself to invoke the grace of the Holy Spirit. Suddenly he began to overflow with eloquence.

—*The Life of St. Francis of Assisi* by St. Bonaventure

Francis and his friends were to the last degree simple in their preaching. His sermons had more of the flavor of exhortations than of elaborated discourses—they were artless words, which came from the heart and went to the heart. His preaching always came back to three points: fear God, love God, convert yourself from bad to good.

—*St. Francis of Assisi* by Johannes Jørgensen

If we do not know exactly what Francis said, witnesses graphically describe how he said it. His idiosyncratic delivery made full use of all his skills as a troubadour. His expression was friendly and cheerful; his voice clear and attractive; eloquent and often witty, he became crisp and fiery when he denounced to their faces men commonly known to be guilty of greed, exploitation and cruelty.

—*Francis of Assisi: A Revolutionary Life* by Adrian House

REMEMBRANCES OF SAINT FRANCIS

When I was a student in Bologna I saw St. Francis preach. . . .
Although no scholar, he spoke so well and developed the subject
of these three classes of rational and spiritual beings so clearly
that he won the unbounded admiration of even the academics
in the crowd. Yet it was more of a general address than a sermon.
He wore a tattered habit, his appearance was insignificant, and
his face wasn't handsome; but God gave his words such power
that they actually restored peace to many of the noble families
long torn apart by hatred, cruelty, and murder. At the same time
ordinary men and women flocked to him out of devotion and
respect, afterwards trying to tear a shred from his habit or at least
to touch him.

—Thomas of Spalato, Archdeacon of Spalato in Dalmatia
   recalls hearing St. Francis in 1222, quoted in *Francis of Assisi:
   A Revolutionary Life* by Adrian House

Blessed Francis, traveling through the cities and towns, set about preaching everywhere; not with the persuasive words of human wisdom, but in keeping with the truth and the power of the Holy Spirit, he confidently announced the Kingdom of God. He was a genuine preacher of the Gospel, strengthened by apostolic authority; he used no flattering phrases and despised the charm of rhetorical devices. For before he tried to convince others by his sermons, he had started by convincing himself, by laboring to proclaim the divine truth with the greatest possible fidelity. The power and truth of his words, which he did not own to any schoolmaster, elicited the admiration of everyone, even the educated and the learned. A great number of them hastened to see and hear him, as though he were a man from another time.

—*The Legend of the Three Companions*

The word of St. Paul, "Be my imitators, as I myself am of Christ" (1 Cor. 11:1), we can with good right put upon the lips of Francis, who, in imitating the Apostle, has become the most faithful image and copy of Jesus Christ.

—Pope Benedict XV

Remembrances of Saint Francis

One night when Blessed Peter Pettinaio of the Third Order was praying in the Cathedral of Siena, he saw Our Lord Jesus Christ enter the church, followed by a great throng of saints. And each time Christ raised his foot, the form of his foot remained imprinted on the ground. And all the saints tried as hard as they could to place their feet in the traces of His footsteps, but none of them was able to do so perfectly. Then St. Francis came in and set his feet right in the footsteps of Jesus Christ.

—*The Little Flowers of St. Francis*

What made me love the life of blessed Francis so much was the fact that it resembled the beginning and growth of the church. As the church began with simple fishermen and afterwards developed to include renowned and skilled doctors, so it was in the case of the order of Francis, showing that it was not founded by the prudence of men, but by Christ.

—*The Life of St. Francis of Assisi* by St. Bonaventure

So radical is Francis' love of Christ that he wants to experience the pain of the Beloved, to be so identified with Christ that he knows "from the inside" what Jesus suffered. Furthermore he is bent on loving God with his whole soul and heart and mind, but his wayward heart keeps revealing itself in the "selfish" demands of his own body. . . . And in one sense Francis appears unreasonable to those of us less smitten. He is a hero in love, his language and actions those of a person whose heart has been wounded by love, who is intoxicated by the perfume of the Beloved. To others the heroic lover always seems a bit mad, someone going through a phase, someone who will eventually pass from the insanity of being in love to the sanity and reasonableness of love. But that does not happen to Francis. He is in love with Jesus Christ all his life, like a young lover who is experiencing for the first time what it means to fall in love.

—*The Way of St. Francis* by Murray Bodo

Who could feel sorry for St. Francis because he threw away his clothes and took the vow of poverty? He was the first man on record, I imagine, who asked for stones instead of bread. Living on the refuse which others threw away he acquired the strength to accomplish miracles, to inspire joy such as few men have given the world, and, by no means the least of his powers, to write the most sublime and simple, the most eloquent hymn of thanksgiving that we have in all literature, "The Canticle of the Sun." Let go and let be! . . . Being is burning, in the truest sense, and if there is to be any peace it will come about through being, not having.

—Henry Miller, quoted in *The Way of St. Francis* by Murray Bodo

The whole point about Saint Francis of Assisi is that he certainly was ascetical, and he certainly was not gloomy.

As soon as ever he had been unhorsed by the glorious humiliation of his vision of dependence on the divine love, he flung himself into fasting and vigil exactly as he had flung himself furiously into battle. He had wheeled his charger clean round, but there was no halt or check in the thundering impetuosity of his charge.

There was nothing negative about it; it was not a regiment or a stoical simplicity of life. It was not self-denial merely in the sense of self-control. It was as positive as pleasure. He devoured fasting as a man devours food. He plunged after poverty as men have dug madly for gold.

—"The Ungloomy Ascetic" by G. K. Chesterton

Francis did his utmost to encourage the friars to lead austere lives, but he had no time for exaggerated self-denial.

—*The Life of St. Francis of Assisi* by St. Bonaventure

St. Francis walked the world like the Pardon of God. I mean that his appearance marked the moment when men could be reconciled not only to God but to nature and, most difficult of all, to themselves.

—*St. Francis of Assisi* by G. K. Chesterton

He strove to bend his own will to the will of God.

—Thomas of Celano

Francis left his mark on the art, literature and history of Western civilization—beginning with Dante, who was born forty years after his death and who devoted to Francis almost an entire canto of the *Commedia*. It is no exaggeration to say that all subsequent Italian expressions of religious culture are indebted to Francis, from the frescoes of Cimabue and Giotto to the films of Vittoria de Sica and Federico Fellini, which are suffused with a deeply Franciscan sensibility.

—*Reluctant Saint* by Donald Spoto

And St. Francis, however wild and romantic his gyrations might appear to many, always hung on to reason by one invisible and indestructible hair.

—*St. Francis of Assisi* by G. K. Chesterton

Francis is like sparkling diamonds, which, from each of their facets, give off splinters that seem to differ according to the way they are struck by the light.

—Raoul Manselli

Francis brought the world a life of radical simplicity, unmoored to possessions and therefore free to follow the promptings of grace and the path toward God, wherever and whenever God summoned him. His spirit was one of remarkable spontaneity: he leaped to the needs of others, just as he hurried to catch up with God, Who was always inviting him to a new adventure. Francis was no theoretician of the spiritual life. He never spoke of God in any but experiential terms, because he was a witness to a living and acting God. He could speak only of what he saw, heard, and felt. In this regard, he remains before us, across the centuries, as an example of what God can do—which is primarily to astonish, to alter radically the way we live and move. In the dramatic passages of his own life, and the remarkable ways in which a genial but rather shallow young playboy became a model of service to the world, he revealed that God is present in time and history. In other words, he has such credibility because he demonstrated that we are at our best when we dare to allow God into our lives.

—*Reluctant Saint* by Donald Spoto

Francis of Assisi, as has been said again and again, was a poet; that is, he was a person who could express his personality. Now it is everywhere the mark of this sort of man that his very limitations make him larger. He is what he is, not only by what he has, but in some degree by what he has not. But the limits that make the lines of such a personal portrait cannot be made the limits of all humanity. St. Francis is a very strong example of this quality in the man of genius, that in him even what is negative is positive, because it is part of a character.

—*St. Francis of Assisi* by G. K. Chesterton

People believed in him. They wanted to believe in the Dream, and he was proof that it was. His name was Francis, and he lived and died quietly and peacefully in Assisi. When the light of the spirit was dying out all over the world, this man, this little man, this one man, re-enkindled the flame. He was only forty-five years old when he died, but he left behind a dream to dream and a journey to challenge every man.

—*The Journey and the Dream* by Murray Bodo

Francis's spirit lives on in extraordinary people today. Standing as we do with the benefit of hindsight, the similarities between the little poor man from Assisi and other notable spiritual figures, such as Mahatma Gandhi, for instance, are many. Despite different religious underpinnings, we can almost see Francis when we see photographs of the sandaled, loin-clothed Gandhi negotiating with the rulers of Europe. In other contexts, Francis has been compared to Dorothy Day, founder of the Catholic Worker movement in twentieth-century America, and Mother Teresa of Calcutta, just to name a few. We each have the capacity to be a saint like him, Francis certainly believed so.

—*The Road to Assisi* by Jon M. Sweeney

Who, then, O greatest of the saints, could imagine and explain to others the ardor of your soul?

—Thomas of Celano

Since I cannot speak much because of my weakness and pain I wish briefly to make my purpose clear to all my brothers present and to come. I wish them always to love one another as I have loved them; let them always love and honor our Lady Poverty; and let them remain faithful and obedient to the bishops and clergy of holy mother church.

—St. Francis's words to his brothers near the end of his life, from *The Legend of Perugia*

I have done what is mine to do; may Christ teach you to do yours.

 —St. Francis on his deathbed

Bring me out of prison
That I may give thanks to Thy name;
The righteous will surround me,
For thou wilt deal bountifully with me.

 —Psalm 142, Francis's last words, from *The First Life of*
  St. Francis by Thomas of Celano

As the morning star in the midst of a cloud, and as the moon
at the full (cf. Ecclus. 50:6), he took in his hands a lamp with
which to draw the humble by the example of his glorious deeds,
and a trumpet wherewith to recall the shameless with stern and
fearsome warnings from their wicked abandon.

 —Pope Gregory IX, The Bull of Canonization of St. Francis
  of Assisi, 1228

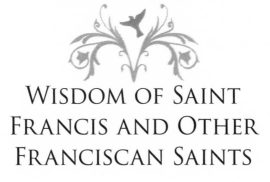

WISDOM OF SAINT FRANCIS AND OTHER FRANCISCAN SAINTS

G od give you His peace.

 —St. Francis's opening to every sermon.

When you have stabilized your heart in right faith, and steadfast hope, and perfect love, then you will heave up your heart in high contemplation of your Creator.

 —St. Francis

In God alone there is primordial and true delight, and in all our delights it is this that we are seeking.

—St. Bonaventure

Our thoughts ought instinctively to fly upwards from animals, men, and natural objects to their Creator. If things created are so full of loveliness, how resplendent with beauty must be He who made them! The wisdom of the Worker is apparent in His handiwork.

—St. Anthony of Padua

No matter how much our interior progress is ordered, nothing will come of it unless by divine aid. Divine aid is available to those who seek it from their hearts, humbly and devoutly; and this means to sigh for it, in this valley of tears, through fervent prayer.

—St. Bonaventure

Take thought now, redeemed man, and consider how great and worthy is He who hangs on the cross for you. His death brings the dead to life, but at his passing heaven and earth are plunged into mourning and hard rocks are split asunder.

—St. Bonaventure

O religious soul, dove beloved of Christ, behold those little pieces of straw which the world tramples under its feet. They are the virtues practiced by the Savior and thy Spouse, of which He Himself has set thee an example: humility, meekness, poverty, penance, patience, and mortification.

—St. Anthony of Padua

Love Him totally Who gave Himself totally for your love.

—St. Clare of Assisi

In all your deeds and words you should look upon this Jesus as your model. Do so whether you are walking or keeping silence, or speaking, whether you are alone or with others. He is perfect, and thus you will be not only irreprehensible, but praiseworthy.

—St. Bonaventure

O name of Mary! Joy in the heart, honey in the mouth, melody to the ear of her devout clients!

—St. Anthony of Padua

Above all the grace and the gifts that Christ gives to his beloved is that of overcoming self.

—St. Francis

But in these days there are many among us who want to win honor and praise from men by merely proclaiming and reciting the deeds of Saints.

—St. Francis, from *The Mirror of Perfection*

The peace you proclaim with words must dwell even more abundantly in your hearts. Do not provoke others to anger or create scandal. Rather, let your gentleness draw them to peace, goodness, and harmony. This is our vocation: to heal wounds, to bind what is broken, to bring home those who are lost.

—St. Francis, *The Legend of the Three Companions*

Blessed are the peacemakers, for they shall be called the children of God (cf. Matt. 5:9). The true peacemakers are those who preserve peace of mind and body for love of our Lord Jesus Christ, despite what they suffer in this world.

—St. Francis, The Admonitions, XV

You ascend more quickly to heaven from a hovel than a palace.

—St. Francis, from *The First Life of St. Francis* by Thomas of Celano

True progress quietly and persistently moves along without notice.

—St. Francis

My Good Shepherd, who have shown Your very gentle mercy to us unworthy sinners in various physical pains and sufferings, give grace and strength to me, Your little lamb, that in no tribulation or anguish or pain may I turn away from You!

—St. Francis, from *The Little Flowers of St. Francis*

He who bears his sufferings with patience for God's sake, will soon arrive at high perfection. He will be master of the world and will already have one foot in the other world.

—St. Giles of Assisi

Gladly endure whatever goes against you and do not let good fortune lift you up: for these things destroy faith.

—St. Clare of Assisi

Our labor here is brief, but the reward is eternal. Do not be disturbed by the clamor of the world, which passes like a shadow. Do not let the false delights of a deceptive world deceive you.

—St. Clare of Assisi

Heaven is not divided by the number of those who reign, nor lessened by being shared, nor disturbed by its multitude, nor disordered by its inequality of ranks, nor changed by motion, nor measured by time.

—St. Bonaventure

Sanctify yourself and you will sanctify society.

—St. Francis

All the darkness in the world can't extinguish the light from a single candle.

—St. Francis, from *The Little Flowers of St. Francis*

Those things that are more scorned and shunned by worldly men are honored and valued by God and His saints. And those that are more loved and embraced and honored by worldly men are more hated and shunned and scorned by God and His saints. Men hate everything that should be loved and love what should be hated.

—St. Giles of Assisi

Poverty is an easy way to God. Poverty is the mother of humility. It is as difficult to preserve humility amid riches as purity in the midst of delights and luxury. Poverty sets free. When a person delights in and gloats over his possessions, in reality he limits, even loses his freedom. The mania of riches has enslaved him. He is lowered in status, being no longer the owner but the owned. He has subordinated himself to his goods. Such servile subjection becomes evident in the fever that dominates him and the anguish that racks him when he loses some of his possessions. In short, true liberty is not found except in voluntary poverty.

—St. Anthony of Padua

If so great and good a Lord, then, on coming into the Virgin's womb, chose to appear despised, needy, and poor in this world, so that people who were in utter poverty and want and in absolute need of heavenly nourishment might become rich in Him by possessing the kingdom of heaven, then rejoice and be glad! Be filled with a remarkable happiness and a spiritual joy! Contempt of the world has pleased You more than its honors, poverty more than earthly riches.

—St. Clare of Assisi

When you have got a psalter you will begin to want to have a breviary. And when you have possessed yourself of a breviary you will sit on a high chair like a great prelate and say to our brother: fetch me my breviary.

—St. Anthony of Padua

Close your ears to the whisperings of hell and bravely oppose its onslaughts.

—St. Clare of Assisi

Since happiness is nothing other than the enjoyment of the highest good and since the highest good is above, no one can be happy unless he rise above himself, not by an ascent of the body, but of the heart.

—St. Bonaventure

Melancholy is the poison of devotion. When one is in tribulation, it is necessary to be more happy and more joyful because one is nearer to God.

—St. Clare of Assisi

Happy is the man whose words issue from the Holy Spirit and not from himself.

—St. Anthony of Padua

Remember: The sinner who is sorry for his sins is closer to God than the just man who boasts of his good works.

—St. Padre Pio

A person who desires perfection needs to undertake both internal and external action. In striving toward internal perfection, we must first practice the virtue of charity. When a person loves money, honors, and good health, he does not always possess what he loves, whereas he who loves God possesses Him at once. Also, the soul needs patience. The virtue of patience maintains order in one's interior life. Love, joy, and peace are virtues which perfect the soul with regard to what it possesses, while patience perfects it with regard to what it endures.

—St. Padre Pio

Love is the first ingredient in the relief of suffering.

—St. Padre Pio

Love, and practice simplicity and humility, and don't worry about the opinion of the world, because if this world had nothing to say against us, we would not be true servants of God.

—St. Padre Pio

Don't spend your energies on things that generate worry, anxiety and anguish. Only one thing is necessary. Lift up your spirit, and love God.

—St. Padre Pio

Don't be upset about those outbursts, although you should never be satisfied with them. If the Lord doesn't give you the grace of inexhaustible and continual gentleness, it is in order to leave you a means to practice holy humility. As a penance, every time you let yourself go, you must show yourself twice as gentle immediately.

—St. Padre Pio

Therefore, O soul, make a daily examination of your life. Look carefully to see how far you have advanced and how much further you have yet to go; look at the quality of your morals and the character of your love; examine to what degree you are like God and to what degree you are unlike God; take note of how close to God, or how far removed from God you are. Remember this always: it is better and more praiseworthy to know yourself than to ignore yourself while you come to know the course of the stars, the power of herbs, the structure of human nature, and the nature of animals—in short, all other things of heaven and earth. Turn to your inner self, if not always, then at least from time to time. Master your affections, guide your actions, correct your ways.

—St. Bonaventure

No pilgrim soul can worthily love God. But when a soul does everything possible and trusts in divine mercy, why would Jesus reject such a spirit? Has He not commanded us to love God according to our strength? If you have given and consecrated everything to God, why be afraid?

—St. Padre Pio

Our body is not made of iron. Our strength is not that of stone. Live and hope in the Lord, and let your service be according to reason. Modify your holocaust with the salt of prudence.

—St. Clare of Assisi

When paradise is poured into a heart, this afflicted, exiled, weak, and mortal heart cannot bear it without weeping.

—St. Padre Pio

Do not ever lose heart when the tempest rages; place all your trust in the Heart of the most gentle Jesus. Pray and I might add, devoutly pester the divine Heart.

—St. Padre Pio

Where there is charity and wisdom, there is neither fear nor ignorance. Where there is patience and humility, there is neither anger nor vexation. Where there is poverty and joy, there is neither greed nor avarice. Where there is peace and meditation, there is neither anxiety nor doubt.

—St. Francis

In all that you do, always be humble, guarding jealously the purity of your heart and the purity of your body; these are the two wings which will raise us to God and make us almost divine.

—St. Padre Pio

Try to serve the Lord with all your heart and with all your will. He will always bless you more than you deserve.

—St. Padre Pio

Walk with simplicity on the road to the Lord, and don't torment your spirit. It is necessary to hate your faults, but do so tranquilly, not fastidiously and uneasily.

—St. Padre Pio

The word of God does not belong to him who hears or speaks it, but to him who puts it into practice.

—St. Giles of Assisi

Society, wounded with the sores of evil, is Lazarus. We are the dogs who must draw near to cure with our tongues—our preaching—by which we lick with the milk and honey of kindness and gentleness, healing not aggravating the evils that afflict humankind.

—St. Anthony of Padua

Let us begin today, my brothers, to do good because until now we have done nothing.

—St. Francis

Start by doing what's necessary; then do what's possible; and suddenly you are doing the impossible.

—St. Francis

Preach always. If necessary use words.

—St. Francis

CHRONOLOGY

1181 — Francis is born in Assisi, baptized Giovanni di Pietro Bernardone, renamed Francesco by his father, Pietro.

1190 to 1195 — Francis attends school at his parish church, San Giorgio.

1197 — Francis begins to work with his father in the cloth trade.

1202 to 1203 — War breaks out between Assisi and Perugia. Assisi is defeated at the Battle of Collestrada, and Francis is taken prisoner. He spends a year imprisoned in a dungeon; contracts either malaria or tuberculosis; and is finally ransomed by his father.

1204 — Francis suffers from a long period of illness.

1205 — Francis joins the army of Walter de Brienne. He falls ill in Spoleto and has a startling vision that marks the beginning of his conversion. He returns to Assisi and attempts to discern his vocation.

1206 — While praying before a crucifix in a church at San Damiano, Francis hears the voice of God imploring him to repair the church. He sells all he owns and his father's wares as well and gives the proceeds to the priest at San Damiano. His father demands restitution before the Bishop of Assisi. Francis gives back the money, renounces his father, and assumes a hermit's habit. He spends his time in prayer, repairing churches, and helping lepers.

1208 — Francis begins to preach penance and is joined by his first brothers, Bernard of Quintavalle and Peter of Cattaneo. Brother Giles joins them thereafter. Their habits are made of rough cloth and are tied at the waist with a rope.

1209 — Francis writes a brief Rule for himself and his eleven friars or brothers.

1210 — They travel to Rome and meet with Pope Innocent III and receive approval for their order.

1209 to 1211 — First preaching tours.

1211 — The community takes the name of Friars Minor and settles in Portiuncula.

1212 — Clare of Assisi enters religious life and the Second Order is established.

1215 — First general chapter meeting in Assisi.

1217 — Missionaries depart for France, England, and Germany.

1219 — First friar missionaries leave for Morocco. Francis sails for the Holy Land and Egypt. Francis meets with the Sultan.

1220 — Friars are killed in Morocco becoming the first Franciscan martyrs.

1220 — Francis resigns as General Minister and Peter of Cattaneo is appointed.

1221 — Peter of Cattaneo dies and Brother Elias becomes the vicar general. The First Rule is written for the friars.

1221 to 1222 — Francis goes on a preaching tour through Italy.

1223 — Francis writes the definitive Rule for the Order of Friars Minor. It is approved by Pope Honorius III.

1223 — Francis constructs what is considered to be the first Christmas crèche at midnight mass in Greccio.

1224 — Francis begins his long retreat at Alvernia. While there, he receives the stigmata, the five wounds of Christ.

1225 — The eye disease Francis contracted in Egypt worsens. He stays for a time with St. Clare and her sisters at San Damiano. He undergoes medical cauterizing that does not give him any relief. Virtually blind, he composes "The Canticle of Brother Sun."

1226 — While at the Bishop's house in Assisi, Francis realizes he is dying and asks to be brought to Portiuncula.

October 3, 1226 — Francis dies in the evening. He is buried the next day in San Giorgio Church.

July 16, 1228 — Pope Gregory IX canonizes Francis.

May 25, 1230 — St. Francis's remains are moved to his tomb in the new Papal Basilica of St. Francis of Assisi in the town of Assisi.